Mastering z/OS Management Facility: A Comprehensive Guide to Mainframe Innovation

Isaac Nangan

Mastering z/OS Management Facility: A Comprehensive Guide to Mainframe Innovation

Mainframes

Isaac Nangan

Published by Isaac Nangan, 2023.

MASTERING Z/OS MANAGEMENT FACILITY: A COMPREHENSIVE GUIDE TO MAINFRAME INNOVATION

First edition. December 6, 2023.

ISBN: 979-8223020585

Written by Isaac Nangan.

Table of Contents

To Coleen, Sky and Neo. You are my inspirations.

Preface

In the world of mainframes, the IBM z/OS operating system remains a stalwart platform, essential for numerous industries across the globe. The z/OS Management Facility (z/OSMF) represents a key piece of this technological juggernaut, a solution designed to simplify, streamline, and modernize z/OS system management. The z/OSMF is not just a part of the story of mainframe innovation—it is pivotal to its future.

The purpose of this book, "Mastering z/OS Management Facility: A Comprehensive Guide to Mainframe Innovation", is to introduce and demystify z/OSMF to a wide range of readers: from the seasoned mainframe professionals looking to adapt to modern management techniques, to the budding enthusiasts wanting to get a foothold in this expansive field.

The book begins by offering an overview and historical perspective of z/OSMF, setting a solid foundation of understanding. We then delve into the architectural structure of z/OSMF, detailing its core components, functions, and services. We believe it's critical for users to understand the backbone of the system they are using, to enable more proficient and efficient usage.

To bridge the gap between theory and practice, the book provides a comprehensive guide on installing, configuring, and verifying z/OSMF, accompanied by plenty of screenshots and step-by-step instructions. It also includes a thorough walkthrough of the z/OSMF interface and a detailed description of how to leverage z/OSMF for effective system management.

As we delve deeper, we explore advanced features such as plug-ins, extensions, capacity provisioning, and the utilization of REST APIs in z/OSMF. These sections cater to readers who wish to harness the full potential of z/OSMF for their mainframe operations.

Security and compliance, vital aspects of any IT operation, get their due attention. Role-based access control and auditing management strategies are discussed to help safeguard your systems and data. Furthermore, the book offers advice for troubleshooting and maintaining z/OSMF, ensuring its smooth operation and long-term efficacy.

Finally, we gaze into the crystal ball, examining the future directions of z/OSMF and what they mean for the broader landscape of mainframe management.

Whether you're a seasoned professional aiming to modernize your skills, a novice just beginning your mainframe journey, or an IT enthusiast interested in understanding the giant that is IBM z/OS, this book aims to be your comprehensive guide to z/OSMF. We've endeavored to present technical complexities in a reader-friendly manner, enabling a deep and nuanced understanding of this key mainframe technology.

Welcome aboard on this journey into the world of z/OSMF. Let's explore and learn together.

Ricardo Nuqui

Prologue

The year was 1964 when IBM first launched System/360, the mainframe that revolutionized the computer industry by introducing compatibility between systems. Over the years, mainframes have evolved dramatically, becoming a cornerstone of today's digital world. Despite the growth of distributed systems and cloud computing, mainframes continue to be relied upon in sectors where high availability, security, and transaction processing are paramount. In short, mainframes remain the backbone of the IT industry.

Yet, managing mainframe systems can be an intricate task. The IBM z/OS operating system, for example, is known for its power and sophistication, but also its complexity. This is where the z/OS Management Facility (z/OSMF) comes into the picture.

Launched by IBM as a web-based interface for managing z/OS, z/OSMF has significantly simplified mainframe management. It brings automation, workflow-driven processes, and a user-friendly interface to the traditionally complex world of z/OS operations. Its influence extends beyond mere operations management, aiding in tasks such as software installation, incident log management, resource allocation, and more.

This book, "Mastering z/OS Management Facility: A Comprehensive Guide to Mainframe Innovation", is a journey through the world of z/OSMF. It is an exploration of its functionalities, its influence, and its impact on the future of mainframe operations. The upcoming chapters aim to provide a comprehensive view of z/OSMF, going from its historical origins and architectural makeup to its practical application and the best practices for use.

As you turn the page, you are not just reading a book - you are embarking on an exciting expedition into the heart of one of the most influential innovations in mainframe history. The story of z/OSMF is a story of transformation, of the continuous evolution of mainframes to meet the demands of a digital age. Welcome to this adventure - let's delve into the extraordinary world of z/OSMF.

Chapter 1: Introduction

1.1 Overview of z/OSMF

z/OS Management Facility (z/OSMF) is a powerful, modern, web-based tool designed by IBM to simplify, automate, and streamline the management and administration of z/OS systems. It offers a graphical user interface (GUI) that provides intuitive, task-oriented workflows, drastically reducing the traditional complexities associated with mainframe operations.

z/OSMF is built on a service-oriented architecture, making use of a variety of web technologies, such as RESTful APIs and JSON data formats. This design allows for flexibility and extensibility, enabling z/OSMF to support a wide range of management tasks. These include (but are not limited to) configuration and administration, software installation, incident log management, workflow creation and automation, and resource allocation.

One of the significant benefits of z/OSMF is its ability to bridge the gap between experienced mainframe professionals and newcomers to the field. Its graphical interface is far more familiar to those who have worked primarily with distributed systems, making the transition to mainframe management less daunting.

1.2 The Importance of z/OSMF

The z/OS operating system powers some of the most critical infrastructures in the world. Banks, healthcare providers, governments, and numerous industries rely on mainframes for their high-speed data processing, robust security, and unparalleled uptime.

Despite these impressive qualities, traditional mainframe management can often be challenging, complex, and not easily accessible to those without a strong mainframe background. The need for a more intuitive, user-friendly, and modern interface to manage mainframe systems is what led to the creation of z/OSMF.

z/OSMF plays a crucial role in contemporary mainframe operations. It allows for a more simplified, efficient, and productive administration of z/OS systems, lowering the barriers of entry for newer mainframe professionals. z/OSMF also reduces the time and effort involved in many management tasks, allowing IT personnel to focus on strategic, value-added work.

As mainframes continue to evolve and adapt to the requirements of a digital age, z/OSMF stands as a testament to IBM's commitment to this evolution. It symbolizes a bridge between the proven reliability of mainframes and the demand for more modern, accessible, and efficient system management tools.

In this book, we will explore in detail the features, functionalities, and applications of z/OSMF, providing you with the knowledge and tools needed to fully leverage this transformative technology.

1.1 Overview of z/OSMF

IBM'S Z/OS MANAGEMENT Facility (z/OSMF) is a product that provides a modern, web-based interface for managing IBM's z/OS systems. It is designed to make system management tasks easier, more efficient, and more intuitive, especially for professionals who may not be experts in traditional mainframe operations.

z/OSMF is not a single tool, but rather a suite of functions bundled together in a simplified and streamlined interface. It provides a graphical user interface (GUI) that can be accessed through a web browser, offering administrators a familiar, easy-to-navigate environment for managing their z/OS systems.

Built upon a service-oriented architecture, z/OSMF is modular and extensible. It supports a broad range of management tasks. Here are some of the key functions provided by z/OSMF:

1. Configuration and Administration: z/OSMF enables administrators to perform a variety of configuration and administration tasks for z/OS systems, such as setting up system parameters and managing system resources.
2. Software Installation: z/OSMF provides features that simplify the process of installing and managing software on z/OS systems. It supports the IBM Packaging Utility and offers a guided workflow for the software installation process.
3. Incident Log Management: z/OSMF's Incident Log function allows administrators to gather diagnostic data and manage problem records. This feature is useful for troubleshooting system issues and collaborating with IBM Support.
4. Workflows: One of the notable features of z/OSMF is the ability to create, manage, and automate workflows. Workflows are sequences of steps designed to perform complex tasks, and they can be created manually or imported

from templates.

5. Resource Allocation: z/OSMF allows for effective resource management, enabling administrators to create, delete, and modify resources such as z/OS UNIX files and directories, data sets, and z/OS data definitions (z/OSMF Datasets and File Systems functions).

These capabilities make z/OSMF a versatile and comprehensive tool for managing z/OS systems. However, it's important to note that the utility of z/OSMF extends beyond the tasks it performs. It plays a significant role in lowering the entry barriers for mainframe operations, making it a crucial tool for the modern mainframe landscape.

1.2 The Importance of z/OSMF

IBM'S Z/OS MANAGEMENT Facility (z/OSMF) plays a pivotal role in the modern mainframe landscape. Its importance can be seen from several perspectives.

Simplifying Mainframe Management

Traditional mainframe management tasks often involve dealing with complex command-line interfaces, extensive manuals, and a steep learning curve. z/OSMF offers a graphical, web-based interface that is more intuitive and user-friendly, simplifying the process of managing mainframe systems. It enables administrators to carry out tasks more efficiently and with less chance of error, leading to a more robust and reliable system.

Bridging the Skills Gap

With many experienced mainframe professionals reaching retirement age, there is a growing concern about a skills gap in the industry. The z/OSMF plays an important role in bridging this gap. Its familiar, browser-based interface and task-oriented workflows make it easier for professionals with less mainframe experience - particularly those accustomed to distributed systems - to effectively manage z/OS environments.

Enhancing Productivity

z/OSMF comes with functionalities that enable the automation of many routine tasks. For instance, its workflows feature allows administrators to create and automate sequences of tasks, reducing manual intervention and the potential for human error. This automation helps IT personnel focus more on strategic tasks, leading to higher productivity and lower operational costs.

Facilitating Modernization and Digital Transformation

As businesses continue to evolve in the digital era, mainframes need to adapt and integrate with new technologies. z/OSMF supports modern web technologies such as RESTful APIs, making it easier for organizations to integrate their mainframes with other systems, platforms, and applications. This facilitates digital transformation efforts and helps maintain the relevancy and competitiveness of mainframes in the modern IT landscape.

In summary, z/OSMF is not just a tool for managing z/OS systems. It is a crucial enabler that simplifies management tasks, bridges the skills gap, enhances productivity, and facilitates modernization. It is instrumental in maintaining the strength and relevancy of mainframes in today's rapidly evolving digital world.

Chapter 2: History of z/OSMF

2.1 Evolution of z/OS Management

z/OS, IBM's flagship operating system for mainframe computers, has a history that spans over half a century. Initially, managing these mainframe systems was a complex task, typically involving command-line interfaces, detailed system knowledge, and direct interaction with the hardware.

As the systems evolved and became more sophisticated, so did the management tools. The primary focus of these tools was to increase the system's stability, efficiency, and throughput. Over time, automation was introduced to simplify repetitive tasks and reduce the possibility of human error.

Despite these advancements, there was still a steep learning curve for managing z/OS systems, particularly for those not well-versed in the intricacies of mainframe operations. The command-line interfaces, while powerful, were not as user-friendly or accessible as the graphical interfaces that were becoming prevalent in personal computers and distributed systems. This disparity created a need for a more modern, user-friendly way to manage z/OS systems.

2.2 The Creation and Evolution of z/OSMF

In response to this need, IBM introduced the z/OS Management Facility (z/OSMF) in the late 2000s. z/OSMF was a significant shift from traditional mainframe management. It was designed as a web-based, graphical interface, making it more intuitive and accessible for a new generation of IT professionals.

Since its initial release, z/OSMF has continuously evolved, with IBM regularly adding new features and functionalities. Early versions focused primarily on basic system management tasks, such as viewing system status and managing system resources. Over time, more complex capabilities were added, including the ability to create and manage workflows, enhanced software management features, and a variety of plugins for managing specific aspects of z/OS systems.

z/OSMF also incorporated modern web technologies, such as RESTful APIs, allowing for easier integration with other systems and applications. It provided a way to "modernize" mainframe management without sacrificing the power and reliability of the z/OS system.

Today, z/OSMF stands as a testament to the ongoing evolution of mainframe management. It reflects IBM's commitment to making mainframe systems more accessible, efficient, and user-friendly, ensuring their relevance and value in the modern IT landscape.

2.1 Evolution of z/OS Management

THE EVOLUTION OF Z/OS management has been a journey of continuous improvement and adaptation to changing technological landscapes and user needs. This journey began with the introduction of IBM's System/360 in the 1960s and has continued through to the present day with the z/OS operating system and the z/OS Management Facility (z/OSMF).

In the early days of mainframe computing, managing systems was a complex and challenging task. Administrators needed to interact directly with hardware and use complex command-line interfaces to perform management tasks. Only a select group of IT professionals with specialized knowledge and training could efficiently navigate these systems.

With the introduction of the Time-Sharing Option (TSO) and Job Control Language (JCL) in the 1970s, the management of mainframe systems became slightly more accessible. These tools enabled administrators to interact with the system software and submit jobs to the mainframe. However, they still demanded a high degree of technical knowledge and expertise.

As mainframes grew more powerful and complex, IBM introduced Systems Network Architecture (SNA) and Virtual Telecommunications Access Method (VTAM) to help manage network communications. Yet, these systems still required a significant amount of manual configuration and administration.

The 1990s saw the advent of more user-friendly interfaces, such as the ISPF (Interactive System Productivity Facility), which provided a text-based, panel-driven interface for managing z/OS. While a step in the right direction, it was not as intuitive or user-friendly as the graphical interfaces becoming common in the world of personal computers.

With the new millennium came the need for a more modern, intuitive, and accessible method for managing mainframes. This demand led to the creation of the z/OS Management Facility (z/OSMF) in the late 2000s. z/OSMF brought a web-based graphical interface to the world of mainframes, providing an environment more familiar to administrators used to working with distributed systems.

The evolution of z/OS management has been about more than just introducing new features or making tasks easier to perform. It's about ensuring that the power of the mainframe is accessible and usable to a wide range of IT professionals. It's a commitment to bridging the gap between the robust capabilities of the mainframe and the ever-changing demands of the IT industry.

2.2 The Creation and Evolution of z/OSMF

THE Z/OS MANAGEMENT Facility (z/OSMF) was born out of a need for a more modern, intuitive, and accessible approach to managing IBM's mainframe systems. As the complexities of the z/OS operating system grew, the traditional command-line interfaces and manual configurations proved to be daunting for newcomers to the mainframe field and cumbersome even for seasoned professionals. IBM recognized the need for an updated approach and, in the late 2000s, introduced z/OSMF.

Creation of z/OSMF

z/OSMF marked a significant shift from traditional mainframe management. It brought the benefits of a web-based, graphical interface to the mainframe world, making it easier to navigate and manage z/OS systems. The initial versions of z/OSMF were focused on providing basic system management functions, such as viewing system status, managing system resources, and browsing log data.

Evolution of z/OSMF

Over the years, IBM has continually updated and expanded z/OSMF's capabilities, reflecting the changing needs of the IT industry and the growing demand for more automated and streamlined system management tools.

Key enhancements included:

1. Workflow Feature: One of the most significant additions was the workflow feature, which allows administrators to define and automate sequences of tasks. This capability has significantly improved efficiency and reduced the potential for errors in complex management operations.
2. Software Management: Enhanced software management capabilities were added to z/OSMF, making it easier to install, update, and manage software on z/OS systems.

3. Plugins: IBM also introduced a variety of plugins that extended z/OSMF's capabilities, enabling administrators to manage specific aspects of z/OS systems, such as network configuration, security settings, and incident logs.
4. Integration with Modern Web Technologies: z/OSMF adopted modern web technologies such as RESTful APIs, enabling easier integration with other applications and systems, and facilitating the development of custom management tools.

Today, z/OSMF continues to evolve, with IBM regularly adding new features and functionalities. The aim is not just to provide a tool for managing z/OS systems, but to create a platform that can adapt to the changing demands of the IT industry, making mainframe systems more accessible and user-friendly for a new generation of IT professionals.

Chapter 3: Understanding z/OSMF Architecture

3.1 Core Components and Functions

To effectively use z/OSMF, it's essential to understand its architectural components and their respective functions. This section will explore the core components of z/OSMF, including its client interface, server components, plugins, and other integral parts. Each component plays a crucial role in enabling the various functionalities of z/OSMF, from managing system resources to defining and executing workflows.

3.2 Understanding z/OSMF Services

At the heart of z/OSMF is a collection of services that handle specific management tasks. These services, such as workflow services, software management services, and incident log services, are the backbone of z/OSMF, providing the functionalities that make z/OSMF a versatile and comprehensive management tool. This section will delve into these services, explaining what they do and how they interact with each other and the rest of the z/OSMF architecture.

3.3 z/OSMF Infrastructure

z/OSMF isn't just a standalone product; it's a part of the larger z/OS infrastructure. It interacts with various other components of the z/OS environment, including the underlying z/OS operating system, the WebSphere Application Server (WAS), and the z/OS Integrated Information Processor (zIIP). This section will discuss how z/OSMF fits into the broader z/OS ecosystem and how it leverages other components to perform its functions. Understanding this will provide insights into how z/OSMF operates and how it can be integrated into your existing z/OS infrastructure.

3.1 Core Components and Functions

UNDERSTANDING THE ARCHITECTURE of z/OSMF begins with grasping the core components and their respective functions. z/OSMF consists of several key components that contribute to its capabilities:

1. z/OSMF Client Interface: The client interface of z/OSMF is web-based, allowing users to interact with the system through a standard web browser. It provides an intuitive, graphical user interface that simplifies management tasks.
2. z/OSMF Server: The server component of z/OSMF runs on IBM's WebSphere Application Server (WAS) on a z/OS system. The server processes requests from the client interface, performs management tasks, and returns results to the client.
3. z/OSMF Core Services: Core services handle specific management tasks within z/OSMF. These tasks include workflow services, software management services, and incident log services, among others. Each service is responsible for a specific function, and users can access these services through the z/OSMF client interface.
4. z/OSMF Plugins: Plugins extend the functionality of z/OSMF by enabling specific features or supporting additional management tasks. For example, there are plugins for network configuration, capacity provisioning, and job monitoring.
5. z/OSMF Workflow Engine: The workflow engine is a vital component of z/OSMF. It allows administrators to create, manage, and automate workflows, which are sequences of steps designed to perform complex tasks. Workflows can be created manually or imported from templates, and the

workflow engine ensures these workflows are correctly executed.

6. IBM SDK for z/OS Java Technology Edition: z/OSMF relies on the IBM SDK for z/OS Java Technology Edition to run Java applications. This component provides a runtime environment for Java applications, enabling them to interact with the z/OS operating system and perform various tasks.
7. REST APIs: z/OSMF also includes REST APIs, which enable programmatic interaction with z/OSMF services. These APIs allow developers to create custom applications or scripts that automate or enhance z/OSMF operations.

These components work together to provide a versatile, efficient, and user-friendly environment for managing z/OS systems. By understanding these components and how they interact, administrators can make the most of the capabilities offered by z/OSMF.

1. z/OSMF Client Interface

THE Z/OS MANAGEMENT Facility (z/OSMF) Client Interface is the primary point of interaction for users with the z/OSMF system. It's designed to be user-friendly, providing a clear and intuitive graphical user interface (GUI) that simplifies the management of z/OS environments.

The client interface is web-based, meaning it can be accessed via a standard web browser. This makes it accessible from any device that has a web browser, providing a level of flexibility and convenience not typically associated with traditional mainframe management interfaces. It also allows for easy collaboration and sharing of data between team members, as users can quickly share URLs pointing to specific pages within the interface.

The z/OSMF client interface consists of a set of graphical panels, which users can navigate to perform various tasks. These panels are organized into functional areas, such as system management, incident log, and workflow, among others. Each functional area corresponds to a specific set of management tasks that users can perform.

In the system management area, for example, users can view information about system resources, monitor system performance, and manage system settings. The workflow area allows users to create, execute, and manage workflows, while the incident log area provides tools for managing system incidents and problem diagnosis.

The client interface is designed to be intuitive, with a layout and operation similar to many other web-based applications. Tasks are generally performed by navigating to the appropriate panel, filling in required information in form fields, and clicking buttons to submit requests or commands.

Overall, the z/OSMF client interface offers a modern, efficient, and user-friendly way to manage z/OS systems. It enables a wide range of management tasks to be performed with ease, making it an essential tool for any z/OS administrator.

2. z/OSMF Server

THE Z/OS MANAGEMENT Facility (z/OSMF) Server plays a crucial role in the z/OSMF architecture. The server-side of z/OSMF operates on IBM's WebSphere Application Server (WAS) within a z/OS environment. Its main function is to process requests coming from the client interface, execute various management tasks, and then return the results or status of these tasks back to the client.

Here's a more detailed look at the z/OSMF Server:

Operating on WAS: IBM's WebSphere Application Server is a robust platform for running enterprise-level applications. It provides the necessary environment for executing the server-side components of z/OSMF. WAS is designed to deliver high performance, security, and reliability, all of which are essential for the management tasks performed by z/OSMF.

Processing Requests: The z/OSMF Server's primary role is to handle requests sent from the client interface. These requests might be related to viewing system status, modifying configurations, or executing a workflow, among other things. The server interprets these requests and initiates the appropriate tasks.

Performing Management Tasks: Once the server receives a request, it carries out the corresponding management task. This could involve interacting with the z/OS operating system or other z/OS components, running a plugin, or accessing a database, among other tasks. The server has the capabilities to perform a wide variety of management tasks, making it a versatile and powerful tool in the z/OSMF architecture.

Returning Results: After the server has completed a task, it communicates the results back to the client interface. This could be a confirmation that a task was completed successfully, data requested by the client, or an error message indicating that a problem occurred. The server ensures that users are kept informed about the status of their requests and the system as a whole.

In summary, the z/OSMF Server is the workhorse of z/OSMF, doing the heavy lifting of processing requests and performing management tasks. Its integration with WAS ensures it has the robust, reliable platform it needs to perform its tasks efficiently and securely.

3. z/OSMF Core Services

THE CORE SERVICES IN the z/OS Management Facility (z/OSMF) are designed to handle specific management tasks. These services provide the functionality that allows z/OSMF to automate, simplify, and streamline mainframe management tasks. Each of these services performs a specific function, and users can access and interact with these services through the z/OSMF client interface.

Here's a more detailed look at some of the core services in z/OSMF:

Workflow Services: Workflow Services are one of the most valuable components of z/OSMF. They allow users to automate complex sequences of tasks by defining workflows. Once a workflow is created, it can be executed, tracked, and managed through the Workflow Services. These services also allow for the import and export of workflows, promoting reusability and sharing.

Software Management Services: These services provide functionality for managing software installed on the z/OS system. This includes tasks such as installing, updating, or deleting software, as well as managing software dependencies. Software Management Services contribute to the simplification of the software lifecycle management on the mainframe.

Incident Log Services: Incident Log Services provide tools for managing system incidents and logs. These services enable users to view, analyze, and manage incident logs, aiding in problem determination and system recovery processes.

Configuration Assistant Services: These services simplify the configuration of various z/OS components by providing a unified interface for managing system settings.

Resource Monitoring Services: These services allow users to monitor the use of system resources and performance in real time, supporting effective system management and capacity planning.

Security Services: Security services provide the capabilities to manage security settings of the z/OS system, including user roles and permissions, thus ensuring the safety and integrity of the system.

By compartmentalizing these specific functions into individual services, z/OSMF maintains a modular structure. This not only ensures that each service can be focused and optimized for its particular task, but it also allows for the easier addition, modification, or removal of services as the software evolves. This design helps to keep z/OSMF versatile, extensible, and adaptable to changing management needs.

4. z/OSMF Plugins

PLUGINS ARE ADDITIONAL components that can be integrated into the z/OS Management Facility (z/OSMF) to extend its functionality and make it even more versatile. By providing specialized features or supporting additional management tasks, plugins help to customize and enhance the management capabilities of z/OSMF. Users can choose to install plugins based on their specific requirements, thus making z/OSMF a more tailored and efficient tool for managing z/OS systems.

Here's a more detailed look at some types of plugins that can be integrated into z/OSMF:

Network Configuration Plugin: This plugin is designed to simplify the management of z/OS network configurations. It provides tools for creating, editing, and managing network resources such as VIPA addresses, stack definitions, and link definitions. The plugin also includes validation features to help ensure that configurations are correct.

Capacity Provisioning Plugin: The capacity provisioning plugin provides tools for managing and automating capacity provisioning on z/OS systems. This includes features for defining capacity provisioning policies, managing capacity pools, and monitoring the usage of system resources. The plugin leverages the capabilities of z/OS Capacity Provisioning Manager to help ensure that system resources are used efficiently.

Job Monitoring Plugin: The job monitoring plugin provides enhanced features for monitoring and managing jobs on z/OS systems. This includes tools for viewing job status, browsing job logs, and controlling job execution. The plugin makes it easier to manage and troubleshoot jobs, thus enhancing system performance and reliability.

Cloud Provisioning and Management Plugin: This plugin provides features for managing private cloud services on z/OS systems. It supports the creation and management of cloud resources and services, as well as the management of user roles and permissions for accessing these resources.

By using plugins, z/OSMF can be extended and customized to meet the specific needs of an organization. Whether it's managing network configurations, provisioning system capacity, monitoring jobs, or managing cloud resources, plugins make z/OSMF a more versatile and powerful tool for managing z/OS systems. Furthermore, the modular nature of plugins allows for easy addition and removal as the system's requirements change, ensuring that z/OSMF remains flexible and adaptable.

5. z/OSMF Workflow Engine

THE WORKFLOW ENGINE is a key component of the z/OS Management Facility (z/OSMF). It's the driving force behind one of the most valuable features of z/OSMF: the ability to create, manage, and automate workflows. Workflows are sequences of steps designed to perform complex tasks, which can significantly simplify and streamline the management of z/OS systems.

Here's a more detailed look at the Workflow Engine:

Creation of Workflows: The Workflow Engine allows administrators to create workflows from scratch. This involves defining a sequence of steps, each of which corresponds to a specific task. These tasks can involve a wide range of operations, such as running a script, issuing a command, or invoking a z/OSMF service. Each step in the workflow can also have associated prerequisites, conditions that must be met before the step can be executed.

Management of Workflows: Once a workflow has been created, the Workflow Engine provides tools for managing it. Administrators can view the status of a workflow, modify its steps, or control its execution. For example, a workflow can be paused, resumed, or stopped at any time. The Workflow Engine also provides features for tracking the progress of workflows and logging their execution, making it easier to monitor and troubleshoot workflows.

Automation of Workflows: The Workflow Engine not only allows workflows to be executed manually, but it also supports the automation of workflows. This means that workflows can be scheduled to run at specific times or in response to specific events. Automating workflows can significantly improve the efficiency of system management, reducing the time and effort required to perform complex tasks.

Use of Workflow Templates: To further streamline the process of creating workflows, the Workflow Engine supports the use of workflow templates. These are pre-defined workflows that can be imported and used as a starting point for creating new workflows. Templates can be shared between users or organizations, promoting reusability and standardization of workflows.

In summary, the z/OSMF Workflow Engine is an incredibly powerful tool for managing z/OS systems. By allowing complex tasks to be broken down into manageable steps, and by providing the ability to automate these steps, the Workflow Engine makes z/OS management more efficient, reliable, and scalable.

6. IBM SDK for z/OS Java Technology Edition

THE IBM SOFTWARE DEVELOPMENT Kit (SDK) for z/OS Java Technology Edition is a crucial component of z/OSMF. It provides a runtime environment that enables Java applications to operate within the z/OS operating system. This component is vital as it allows z/OSMF, which is largely written in Java, to run efficiently and interact with various parts of the z/OS environment.

Here's a more detailed look at the IBM SDK for z/OS Java Technology Edition:

Java Runtime Environment: The IBM SDK provides a Java Runtime Environment (JRE) for z/OS. This JRE is a subset of the IBM SDK that contains everything required to run Java applications, including the Java Virtual Machine (JVM), the Java core classes, and supporting files. The JVM enables Java applications to run on z/OS systems, interpreting the Java bytecode into instructions that the z/OS system can understand and execute.

Interaction with z/OS: The IBM SDK for z/OS Java Technology Edition enables Java applications to interact with the z/OS operating system and perform various tasks. This can include tasks like reading from and writing to z/OS datasets, invoking z/OS system services, and handling z/OS system events.

Support for Java Applications: The IBM SDK not only provides the runtime environment for Java applications but also supports the development of Java applications for z/OS. It includes a variety of development tools and libraries that can be used to write, debug, and optimize Java applications for z/OS. It also supports the latest Java technologies, ensuring that z/OSMF can leverage the full capabilities of the Java language.

Integration with z/OSMF: Given that z/OSMF is a Java-based application, the IBM SDK for z/OS Java Technology Edition is an integral component of the z/OSMF architecture. It provides the foundation that allows z/OSMF to run on z/OS systems and perform its various management tasks.

In summary, the IBM SDK for z/OS Java Technology Edition plays a vital role in the operation of z/OSMF. By providing a runtime environment for Java applications and enabling these applications to interact with the z/OS system, the IBM SDK ensures that z/OSMF can function efficiently and effectively on z/OS systems.

7. REST APIs

THE REPRESENTATIONAL State Transfer (REST) Application Programming Interfaces (APIs) in z/OS Management Facility (z/OSMF) provide a robust and flexible method for programmatic interaction with z/OSMF services. These APIs offer developers the ability to create custom applications or scripts that can automate or further optimize the operations of z/OSMF.

Let's delve deeper into the importance and role of REST APIs in z/OSMF:

Programmatic Interaction: REST APIs provide a structured way for programs to interact with z/OSMF services. They define the set of actions (or methods) that a program can perform, such as retrieving system information (GET), updating system configurations (PUT), or initiating workflows (POST). This makes it possible for custom applications or scripts to use z/OSMF services programmatically, enhancing the flexibility and utility of z/OSMF.

Automation of Operations: By enabling programmatic access to z/OSMF services, REST APIs open up the possibility of automating operations. For example, a script could be written to automatically initiate a workflow in response to a specific event or to periodically update a system configuration. This can reduce manual effort, improve system response time, and enhance the overall efficiency of z/OS management.

Customization and Integration: REST APIs provide a means for customizing and extending the functionality of z/OSMF. Developers can write custom applications that leverage z/OSMF services to provide new functionality or to better integrate z/OSMF with other systems or processes. This ensures that z/OSMF can be adapted to the specific needs and workflows of an organization.

Platform Independence: One of the key benefits of REST APIs is that they are platform-independent. They use standard HTTP(S) protocols and data formats (like JSON or XML), which are widely supported across different programming languages and platforms. This means that applications or scripts that interact with z/OSMF can be written in virtually any language and run on any platform that supports these standards.

In summary, the inclusion of REST APIs in z/OSMF greatly enhances its versatility and adaptability. They allow for increased automation, customization, and integration, ensuring that z/OSMF can be effectively utilized in a wide variety of contexts and workflows.

3.2 Understanding z/OSMF Services

Z/OS MANAGEMENT FACILITY (z/OSMF) Services are the underlying functions that enable z/OSMF to perform its management tasks. These services are categorized into various types, each designed to handle specific tasks or processes.

Here's a more detailed look at some key types of z/OSMF Services:

1. Workflow Services: Workflow Services enable users to automate sequences of tasks, improving efficiency and minimizing the potential for human error. Users can create, import, export, and manage workflows that can execute numerous tasks such as system setup, software installation, and system checks, among others.

2. Incident Log Services: These services manage system incidents and logs. They assist with problem determination and system recovery processes by allowing users to view, analyze, and manage incident logs.

3. Software Management Services: These services handle the management of software installed on the z/OS system. They perform tasks such as installing, updating, or deleting software, as well as managing software dependencies.

4. Resource Monitoring Services: These services monitor the use of system resources and performance in real time, supporting effective system management and capacity planning.

5. Configuration Assistant Services: These services simplify the configuration of various z/OS components by providing a unified interface for managing system settings.

6. Security Services: These services manage the security settings of the z/OS system, including user roles and permissions, helping to ensure the safety and integrity of the system.

7. Cloud Provisioning Services: These services allow for quick and efficient provisioning of resources in a cloud environment. Users can automate and manage the lifecycle of cloud resources directly from z/OSMF.

8. REST APIs: REST APIs (Application Programming Interfaces) allow external applications to interact programmatically with z/OSMF, opening up more possibilities for automation, integration, and customization.

Understanding z/OSMF Services is crucial to leveraging the full potential of z/OSMF. Each service offers specific functionalities that can greatly simplify and streamline the management of z/OS systems. These services are designed to work in harmony, providing a robust, flexible, and efficient toolset for managing and automating a wide range of tasks on z/OS systems.

1. Workflow Services

WORKFLOW SERVICES FORM a crucial part of z/OS Management Facility (z/OSMF). They empower users to automate sequences of tasks or processes, thereby enhancing efficiency and minimizing the scope of human error. These services deal with workflows, which are a defined series of steps meant to execute a specific task or set of tasks.

Here's a more detailed look at Workflow Services:

Creation of Workflows: Workflow Services allow users to create workflows within z/OSMF. This process involves defining a sequence of tasks that need to be executed to achieve a particular outcome. Each task in the sequence can be assigned specific inputs, prerequisites, and success criteria, ensuring a robust and controlled execution process.

Management of Workflows: Beyond just creating workflows, Workflow Services provide comprehensive management capabilities. Users can modify workflows by adding, removing, or altering tasks. They can also monitor the progress of workflow execution, pause, resume, or stop workflows, and view detailed logs for troubleshooting or auditing purposes.

Import and Export of Workflows: Workflow Services allow users to import and export workflows. This feature facilitates reusability of workflows across different systems or environments, and promotes sharing of workflows among different teams or users. Exported workflows can serve as templates for creating new workflows, saving time and effort.

Automation of Tasks: The core advantage of Workflow Services is the automation they provide. By defining workflows, users can automate complex tasks like system setup, software installation, system checks, and much more. Once a workflow is defined, it can be executed any number of times, reducing manual effort and improving consistency and reliability of operations.

User Interaction and Approval Steps: Workflow Services also support user interaction and approval steps within workflows. These steps can pause the execution of a workflow until a user provides necessary input or approves the continuation of the workflow, adding a layer of control and oversight.

In summary, Workflow Services in z/OSMF provide a powerful tool for automating and managing tasks on z/OS systems. They streamline operations, improve efficiency, and reduce human error, making them an invaluable part of z/OS management.

2. Incident Log Services

INCIDENT LOG SERVICES are an essential part of the z/OS Management Facility (z/OSMF). These services manage system incidents and logs, and they play a critical role in diagnosing problems and aiding system recovery processes.

Let's look at these services more closely:

Incident Recording: The first step in handling system incidents is recording them. When an incident occurs, Incident Log Services capture relevant details such as the time of the incident, the system or component involved, the nature of the incident, and any error messages or codes. This information is stored in an incident log for later analysis.

Incident Viewing: Incident Log Services provide an interface for users to view incident logs. This includes not only the details of each incident but also a summary view showing all recorded incidents. This overview can be helpful in identifying patterns or trends in system incidents, such as recurring issues or spikes in incidents at certain times.

Incident Analysis: Once incidents are recorded and viewed, the next step is analysis. Incident Log Services include tools for analyzing incident logs, such as filtering and sorting capabilities and the ability to drill down into the details of individual incidents. This analysis can help identify the root cause of incidents and guide corrective action.

Problem Determination: By analyzing incident logs, Incident Log Services assist in problem determination. This process involves identifying the cause of an incident, whether it's a software bug, a hardware failure, a configuration error, or some other issue. Incident Log Services can also suggest potential solutions or workarounds for the identified problems.

System Recovery: After the cause of an incident is identified and a solution is proposed, the next step is system recovery. Incident Log Services can help guide this process, providing instructions for correcting issues or recovering from incidents. In more severe cases, these services can also assist in coordinating recovery efforts and tracking progress towards system restoration.

In summary, Incident Log Services play a crucial role in managing system incidents and supporting problem determination and system recovery efforts. By providing a structured and efficient way to record, view, analyze, and manage incident logs, these services can help maintain system stability and reduce downtime.

3. Software Management Services

SOFTWARE MANAGEMENT Services form a fundamental component of the z/OS Management Facility (z/OSMF). They oversee the handling of software installed on the z/OS system and perform a variety of tasks including software installation, updates, deletions, and dependency management.

Here's a closer look at Software Management Services:

Software Installation: These services facilitate the process of installing new software onto the z/OS system. This involves transferring software packages to the system, configuring necessary settings, and performing initial setup tasks. The services can automate much of this process, reducing the potential for human error and improving efficiency.

Software Updates: Keeping software up to date is crucial for security, performance, and access to new features. Software Management Services manage the process of updating software on the z/OS system. They can check for available updates, download and install these updates, and manage any necessary system changes or restarts.

Software Deletion: When software is no longer needed, Software Management Services can handle the deletion process. This involves removing the software from the system, cleaning up any associated files or settings, and ensuring that the system remains stable and functional after the deletion.

Software Dependency Management: Many software applications depend on other software to function correctly. Software Management Services help manage these dependencies, ensuring that all required software is installed and correctly configured. If an update or deletion affects a dependency, the services can alert the user and help resolve the issue.

Software Inventory Management: Apart from the operations on individual software applications, Software Management Services also maintain an inventory of all software installed on the z/OS system. This inventory can provide a quick overview of the software environment and can be useful for troubleshooting, planning updates, or auditing software usage.

In summary, Software Management Services in z/OSMF provide comprehensive management of the software environment on a z/OS system. By automating many common software management tasks, these services can greatly simplify the process of maintaining a stable, secure, and up-to-date software environment on z/OS systems.

4. Resource Monitoring Services

RESOURCE MONITORING Services are vital services within the z/OS Management Facility (z/OSMF). These services monitor the use of system resources and performance in real-time, playing a key role in effective system management and capacity planning.

Here's a more in-depth exploration of Resource Monitoring Services:

Real-time Monitoring: The main function of Resource Monitoring Services is to provide real-time monitoring of system resources. These resources include CPU usage, memory utilization, disk space, network bandwidth, and more. The services continuously track the usage of these resources, providing up-to-date data to system administrators.

Performance Metrics: Alongside monitoring resource usage, Resource Monitoring Services also track performance metrics. This can include metrics such as system load, response time, transaction rates, and more. These metrics can help identify performance bottlenecks and guide optimization efforts.

Alerting: Resource Monitoring Services can also alert administrators to potential issues. For example, if resource usage exceeds a predefined threshold, the services can send an alert to notify administrators. This allows for proactive management of system resources and can help prevent issues before they impact system performance.

Historical Data and Trend Analysis: In addition to real-time data, Resource Monitoring Services also collect and store historical resource usage and performance data. This data can be used to analyze trends over time, such as increasing resource usage or decreasing performance. This trend analysis can inform capacity planning and system optimization efforts.

Reporting: To make the collected data more accessible, Resource Monitoring Services provide reporting features. These can include visual reports, such as graphs or charts, as well as detailed tabular reports. These reports make it easier to understand resource usage and performance data and can support decision-making processes.

In summary, Resource Monitoring Services in z/OSMF provide a comprehensive toolset for monitoring and managing system resources and performance. By providing real-time data, alerting capabilities, and reporting features, these services support effective system management and capacity planning on z/OS systems.

5. Configuration Assistant Services

CONFIGURATION ASSISTANT Services are integral components of the z/OS Management Facility (z/OSMF). These services simplify the configuration of various z/OS components by providing a unified interface for managing system settings.

Let's delve into these services in greater detail:

Unified Configuration Management: One of the key functions of Configuration Assistant Services is to provide a unified interface for managing the configuration of various z/OS components. This interface brings together configuration options for different parts of the system, making it easier to manage and understand the overall system configuration.

System Settings Management: Configuration Assistant Services allow for management of a wide range of system settings. This can include settings for system security, networking, storage, user accounts, and more. Administrators can view current settings, make changes, and apply new settings, all from a single interface.

Configuration Templates: To facilitate and standardize configuration, Configuration Assistant Services provide support for configuration templates. These templates define a set of configuration settings that can be applied to a system or component. Templates can simplify the configuration process and help ensure consistency across multiple systems.

Configuration Validation: After changes are made to a system configuration, it's important to validate these changes to ensure they don't introduce issues. Configuration Assistant Services include features for validating configuration changes, such as checking for conflicts or inconsistencies.

Configuration Auditing: In addition to managing and validating configuration, Configuration Assistant Services also support configuration auditing. This involves tracking changes to system configuration, who made these changes, and when they were made. This audit trail can be useful for troubleshooting, compliance, and security purposes.

In summary, Configuration Assistant Services in z/OSMF provide a powerful and flexible tool for managing z/OS system configuration. By providing a unified interface, supporting configuration templates, and offering validation and auditing features, these services can greatly simplify and improve the process of configuring z/OS systems.

6. Security Services

SECURITY SERVICES FORM a crucial element of the z/OS Management Facility (z/OSMF). These services oversee the management of the z/OS system's security settings, including user roles and permissions. They play a vital role in maintaining the system's safety and integrity.

Let's examine Security Services in more detail:

User Roles and Permissions Management: One of the core functions of Security Services is the management of user roles and permissions. This involves defining what actions each user or role can perform on the z/OS system. The services enable administrators to create roles, assign users to these roles, and manage the permissions associated with each role.

Authentication and Authorization: Security Services also handle authentication and authorization. Authentication verifies the identity of a user, typically through a username and password, while authorization determines what an authenticated user is allowed to do. These services ensure that only authorized users can access the system and perform actions within their permissions.

Security Configuration Management: Security Services manage various security-related configuration settings on the z/OS system. This can include settings for password policies, encryption settings, firewall rules, and more. Changes to these settings can be applied, validated, and audited through the services.

Audit Logging: Security Services also handle audit logging. This involves keeping a record of security-related events on the system, such as logins, configuration changes, and security incidents. These logs can be used for troubleshooting, compliance, and security investigations.

Security Incident Response: When a security incident occurs, such as an unauthorized access attempt, Security Services help manage the response. This can involve blocking the source of the incident, alerting administrators, and guiding the investigation and recovery process.

In summary, Security Services in z/OSMF provide comprehensive security management for z/OS systems. They help manage user roles and permissions, handle authentication and authorization, manage security configuration, and respond to security incidents. By doing so, they play a crucial role in maintaining the safety and integrity of z/OS systems.

7. Cloud Provisioning Services

CLOUD PROVISIONING Services are a significant part of the z/OS Management Facility (z/OSMF). They allow for quick and efficient provisioning of resources in a cloud environment, enabling users to automate and manage the lifecycle of cloud resources directly from z/OSMF.

Here's a closer examination of Cloud Provisioning Services:

Resource Provisioning: At its core, Cloud Provisioning Services facilitate the process of allocating and setting up cloud resources. This could involve provisioning compute resources, storage, databases, or other cloud services. The services allow administrators to define the resources required and manage the provisioning process from within z/OSMF.

Lifecycle Management: Beyond initial provisioning, Cloud Provisioning Services also handle the ongoing management of provisioned resources. This includes starting, stopping, and monitoring resources, as well as managing any necessary updates or configuration changes.

Automated Workflows: Cloud Provisioning Services enable users to define automated workflows for common provisioning tasks. This allows for a more efficient, repeatable, and error-free process, as the tasks can be performed consistently each time according to the workflow.

Service Catalog: A service catalog can be used to standardize and simplify the provisioning process. The catalog contains pre-defined configurations for various types of resources, which users can select when provisioning. This helps ensure consistency, improve efficiency, and reduce the potential for error.

Monitoring and Reporting: As part of the lifecycle management, Cloud Provisioning Services also provide monitoring and reporting features. These can track the usage and performance of provisioned resources, alerting administrators to potential issues and helping to inform capacity planning and performance optimization efforts.

In summary, Cloud Provisioning Services in z/OSMF provide a comprehensive set of capabilities for managing resources in a cloud environment. By streamlining the provisioning process, automating common tasks, and providing ongoing lifecycle management, these services can significantly improve the efficiency and effectiveness of cloud resource management on z/OS systems.

8. REST APIs

REST APIS, OR REPRESENTATIONAL State Transfer Application Programming Interfaces, are a crucial part of the z/OS Management Facility (z/OSMF). They allow external applications to interact programmatically with z/OSMF, enabling a wider range of automation, integration, and customization possibilities.

Let's delve deeper into the role and functioning of REST APIs in z/OSMF:

Programmatic Interaction: The primary role of REST APIs is to enable programmatic interaction with z/OSMF. This means that instead of interacting with z/OSMF through its user interface, applications can communicate directly with z/OSMF by sending HTTP requests to its APIs. This opens up the possibility of automating tasks, integrating with other systems, and customizing the use of z/OSMF.

Automation: REST APIs enable the automation of tasks within z/OSMF. By making API calls, applications can perform tasks such as creating workflows, managing software, and monitoring resources without human intervention. This can greatly improve efficiency and consistency, especially for repetitive tasks.

Integration: REST APIs also facilitate integration between z/OSMF and other systems. For instance, a system monitoring tool could use the APIs to retrieve performance data from z/OSMF, or a configuration management tool could use the APIs to apply configuration changes. This allows for a more unified and streamlined IT management process.

Customization: With REST APIs, organizations can customize the way they use z/OSMF. They can build custom applications or scripts that use the APIs to perform tasks in a way that meets their specific needs. This could involve combining multiple API calls, adding custom logic, or integrating with other tools and services.

Standardized Communication: REST APIs use a standardized, platform-independent communication protocol (HTTP or HTTPS). This means they can be used by applications running on any platform and written in any programming language that supports HTTP. This makes them highly versatile and widely compatible.

In summary, REST APIs in z/OSMF provide a powerful and flexible interface for programmatic interaction with z/OSMF. They unlock numerous possibilities for automation, integration, and customization, making them a key enabler of more efficient and tailored z/OS management.

3.3 z/OSMF Infrastructure

THE Z/OS MANAGEMENT Facility (z/OSMF) Infrastructure refers to the underlying technological framework that supports the functioning and operations of z/OSMF. This includes several interconnected elements, such as:

1. Mainframe Hardware: z/OSMF runs on IBM's z Series mainframes, powerful enterprise-grade computers designed for high-volume, high-transaction-rate applications. The specific hardware configuration can vary depending on the organization's needs, but it typically includes processors, memory, storage devices, and networking hardware.

2. z/OS Operating System: z/OS is the operating system that runs on the mainframe hardware and provides the foundation for z/OSMF. It's a highly secure and scalable operating system designed to support large-scale, mission-critical applications.

3. WebSphere Application Server (WAS): z/OSMF is hosted on IBM's WebSphere Application Server, which is a software framework that hosts Java-based web applications. WAS provides the runtime environment for z/OSMF, handling tasks like request processing, session management, and security.

4. Java Runtime Environment: z/OSMF is a Java-based application, and it requires a Java Runtime Environment (JRE) to execute its Java code. The JRE is provided by IBM's SDK Java Technology Edition, which is specifically designed for running Java applications on z/OS.

5. z/OSMF Core Services: These are the software components that provide the core functionality of z/OSMF, as described in previous sections. They include services for workflow management, software management, incident logging, resource monitoring, and more.

6. z/OSMF Plugins: Plugins extend the functionality of z/OSMF, enabling additional features and services. These plugins could be provided by IBM, third-party vendors, or developed in-house.

7. REST APIs: As mentioned before, z/OSMF includes REST APIs that allow external applications to interact programmatically with z/OSMF.

8. Network Infrastructure: Lastly, the z/OSMF infrastructure also includes the network infrastructure that connects the z/OSMF server to its clients. This typically includes routers, switches, firewalls, and other network devices.

In summary, the z/OSMF infrastructure encompasses a wide range of hardware and software components, all working together to provide a robust, scalable, and flexible environment for managing z/OS systems.

1. Mainframe Hardware

THE Z/OS MANAGEMENT Facility (z/OSMF) is hosted on IBM's z Series mainframes. These are high-capacity, enterprise-grade computer systems known for their superior performance, security, and reliability, making them ideal for high-volume, high-transaction-rate applications.

Here's a closer look at some of the key components of mainframe hardware:

Processors: IBM's z Series mainframes are equipped with powerful processors that can handle a large number of concurrent tasks. These processors are designed for high-speed computation, allowing the mainframe to process large volumes of data quickly and efficiently. Some IBM mainframes use a technology called Parallel Sysplex, which allows multiple processors to work together, further enhancing performance.

Memory: Mainframe systems come with significant amounts of memory (or RAM). This memory is used to store data that's currently being processed, which speeds up operations by providing quick access to this data. The large amounts of memory in mainframe systems allow them to handle large, complex workloads.

Storage Devices: Mainframe systems have access to a variety of storage devices, both internal and external. These can include traditional hard drives, solid-state drives (SSDs), and various forms of network-attached storage. The choice of storage devices can impact the system's performance, capacity, and cost.

Networking Hardware: IBM's z Series mainframes also include advanced networking hardware to facilitate fast, secure communication between the mainframe and other systems. This can include ethernet adapters, fibre channel adapters for connecting to storage area networks (SANs), and more. Some mainframes also support advanced networking features, such as high-speed interconnects for linking multiple mainframes together.

Peripheral Devices: Depending on the specific needs and configuration of an organization, the mainframe hardware may also include various peripheral devices. These could include tape drives for backup, specialized hardware for cryptographic operations, printers, and more.

In summary, IBM's z Series mainframes are robust, high-capacity systems that are well-suited to host z/OSMF. Their hardware configuration can be tailored to the needs of each organization, ensuring the right balance of performance, capacity, and cost.

2. z/OS Operating System

Z/OS IS THE PRIMARY operating system used on IBM mainframes, providing a robust and scalable platform for running a wide range of large-scale, mission-critical applications. It is specially designed for high performance, reliability, security, and scalability, making it the ideal choice for enterprises that need to process vast amounts of data with high transaction rates. Let's delve deeper into the key characteristics and functionalities of the z/OS operating system:

Performance and Scalability: z/OS is designed to maximize the utilization of system resources and deliver high levels of performance, even under heavy workloads. It supports the execution of thousands of concurrent tasks and can easily scale to manage increasing demands without a significant drop in performance. This makes z/OS ideal for large-scale, mission-critical applications.

Reliability and Availability: z/OS provides numerous features designed to ensure system reliability and high availability. This includes advanced error detection and correction capabilities, system recovery tools, and the ability to perform many system maintenance tasks without needing to take the system offline (a feature known as concurrent maintenance).

Security: z/OS provides a highly secure operating environment, with built-in security features such as multi-level security controls, extensive auditing capabilities, and cryptographic features for data protection. It's compliant with key industry security standards, and it supports the secure execution of transactions and data processing tasks.

Workload Management: One of the standout features of z/OS is its sophisticated workload management capabilities. It can automatically prioritize tasks based on predefined business priorities, ensuring that the most important tasks get the resources they need to execute quickly.

Interoperability: Although z/OS is primarily designed to run on IBM mainframe hardware, it offers extensive interoperability features. This allows z/OS to interact and exchange data with other systems and platforms, supporting a diverse IT environment.

Support for Modern Programming Models: In addition to traditional mainframe programming languages like COBOL and PL/I, z/OS also supports modern languages such as Java, Python, and Node.js. This makes it easier to develop and deploy modern applications on the mainframe.

In summary, z/OS is a highly robust and capable operating system, uniquely designed for the mainframe environment. It provides a solid foundation for running the z/OS Management Facility (z/OSMF), contributing to its performance, scalability, and security.

3. WebSphere Application Server (WAS)

IBM'S WEBSPHERE APPLICATION Server, commonly referred to as WAS, is a Java EE (Enterprise Edition) application server that provides a secure and flexible foundation for hosting and running web applications and services. z/OSMF is a web-based application hosted on WAS, where it gets its runtime environment.

Here are some key features and functionalities of WAS:

Java EE Support: WAS fully supports the Java EE platform, enabling you to develop and deploy enterprise-level applications that adhere to the Java EE standards. It provides a comprehensive runtime environment for these applications, ensuring compatibility with various Java technologies such as Servlets, JavaServer Pages (JSP), Enterprise JavaBeans (EJB), and more.

Scalability and Performance: WAS is built to accommodate large-scale applications that need to handle high volumes of data and traffic. It provides features for load balancing and failover, ensuring smooth performance even under heavy load. It also has robust memory management and efficient request processing capabilities, which contribute to its high performance.

Security: WAS includes robust security features to help protect applications and data. This includes support for SSL/TLS for secure data transmission, user authentication and authorization mechanisms, and security policy enforcement. It also provides advanced features like single sign-on (SSO) and support for multiple security standards.

Session Management: WAS provides session management capabilities that help maintain state information across multiple requests from the same user. This is especially useful in web applications, where HTTP, the underlying protocol, is stateless.

Integration Capabilities: WAS is designed to integrate well with other IBM products and third-party systems. It can interact with databases, messaging services, and transaction management systems, among others.

Administration and Management: WAS provides tools for managing and monitoring the server and its applications. This includes a web-based administrative console, command-line tools, and APIs for programmatically managing the server.

In the context of z/OSMF, WAS serves as the platform where the z/OSMF application runs, providing the necessary Java runtime environment and handling important tasks like request processing, session management, and security enforcement.

4. Java Runtime Environment

THE JAVA RUNTIME ENVIRONMENT (JRE) is a software layer that provides the resources necessary for running Java applications. It is part of the Java Development Kit (JDK), but can also be distributed separately. The JRE interprets compiled Java binary code (called bytecode) for the computer's processor so the Java program can be executed.

Key components of the JRE include:

Java Virtual Machine (JVM): At the core of the JRE is the Java Virtual Machine. The JVM is an abstract computing machine that enables a computer to run a Java program. It does this by executing bytecode, providing an extra level of abstraction that allows Java programs to be platform-independent.

Java Class Libraries: These are pre-built Java code libraries providing extensive functionality for various tasks, such as network communication, file I/O, database connection, user interface design, and more. These libraries are a significant part of what makes Java such a powerful and versatile programming language.

Runtime Libraries: The runtime libraries are the code libraries used by the JVM during the execution of a program. They contain many methods that allow the program to interact with the system resources.

In the case of z/OSMF, it uses the IBM SDK Java Technology Edition to provide the Java Runtime Environment. The IBM SDK Java Technology Edition is a product from IBM that features a JRE specifically designed to support applications running on IBM systems, including z/OS. This JRE includes several optimizations and extensions that improve the performance, security, and compatibility of Java applications running on z/OS.

In summary, the JRE is an essential part of the infrastructure that supports z/OSMF. It enables z/OSMF's Java code to be executed, and the specific version provided by the IBM SDK Java Technology

Edition ensures that z/OSMF can leverage the unique features and capabilities of the z/OS platform.

5. z/OSMF Core Services

Z/OS MANAGEMENT FACILITY'S (z/OSMF) core services are software components that enable the platform to deliver its main functionality. These services are designed to simplify various aspects of managing z/OS systems, each focusing on a specific area of system management. Let's delve into these key services:

Workflow Services: These are central to z/OSMF's capability to automate system management tasks. A workflow in this context is a predefined sequence of steps designed to accomplish a specific task, such as setting up a system or installing software. The Workflow Services allow users to create, import, manage, and execute these workflows, making it easier to automate complex tasks and reduce the risk of errors.

Software Management Services: These services streamline the process of managing software on z/OS systems. This includes installing new software, updating existing software, and deleting software. They can also manage software dependencies, ensuring that all required software components are available and correctly installed.

Incident Log Services: Incident Log Services are designed to simplify the process of managing system incidents. They allow users to view, analyze, and manage incident logs, helping with problem determination and system recovery. By making it easier to manage incident logs, these services can help reduce system downtime and improve overall system reliability.

Resource Monitoring Services: Resource monitoring is a crucial aspect of system management, and these services provide tools for monitoring the use of system resources in real time. This can help administrators understand how system resources are being used, identify potential problems before they impact system performance, and plan for capacity needs.

Configuration Assistant Services: Managing the configuration of z/OS components can be complex, but the Configuration Assistant Services provide a unified interface for managing system settings. This can simplify configuration management tasks and reduce the risk of configuration errors.

Cloud Provisioning Services: As more organizations turn to cloud environments for their IT needs, the Cloud Provisioning Services in z/OSMF can simplify the process of provisioning resources in a cloud environment. Users can automate and manage the lifecycle of cloud resources directly from z/OSMF.

Each of these services plays a key role in z/OSMF, contributing to its goal of simplifying and automating z/OS system management. The core services work together, each focusing on a specific area of system management to provide a comprehensive, unified management solution.

6. z/OSMF Plugins

Z/OS MANAGEMENT FACILITY (z/OSMF) plugins are additional software components that extend the platform's core functionality, providing added services and features. The beauty of plugins is that they allow for the expansion of z/OSMF capabilities without altering its core structure. Here's an overview of the role they play:

1. Feature Enhancement: Plugins can introduce new features that expand the capabilities of z/OSMF. For instance, a plugin could add a new interface for monitoring network traffic, a new tool for managing database connections, or an improved visualizer for system performance data.

2. Service Extension: Some plugins may extend existing services by adding new functionalities. For example, a plugin could provide additional options for managing workflows, enhance incident logging with more detailed information, or improve resource monitoring with advanced analytic capabilities.

3. Third-Party Integration: Plugins can facilitate the integration of third-party software with z/OSMF, enabling users to manage these applications directly from the z/OSMF interface. These could include tools for data management, security, system performance, or other aspects of system administration.

4. Customization: Since plugins can be developed by any party (including in-house development teams), they provide a mechanism for customizing z/OSMF to meet specific organizational needs. If the available IBM or third-party plugins do not provide the necessary functionality, an organization can develop its own plugin to address its unique requirements.

In summary, z/OSMF plugins provide a way to extend and tailor the capabilities of the z/OS Management Facility. Whether they're provided by IBM, third-party vendors, or developed in-house, these plugins add significant versatility to the platform, making it a flexible tool for managing z/OS systems.

7. REST APIs in z/OSMF

REST (REPRESENTATIONAL State Transfer) APIs (Application Programming Interfaces) are a set of rules and conventions for building and interacting with web services. REST APIs provide a method for external applications to interact with a service (in this case, z/OS Management Facility or z/OSMF) over HTTP/HTTPS, using standard HTTP methods like GET, POST, PUT, DELETE, and others.

In the context of z/OSMF, these REST APIs offer a programmable interface that lets developers:

1. Automation: Automate routine tasks and processes by scripting calls to the z/OSMF services. This can save time, improve efficiency, and reduce the risk of human error.

2. Integration: Integrate z/OSMF with other systems and applications. This could be used, for example, to incorporate z/OS management tasks into a centralized IT management dashboard, or to tie z/OS operations into an organization's DevOps pipeline.

3. Customization: Customize the behavior of z/OSMF to better suit an organization's specific needs. For example, an organization could use the APIs to build custom user interfaces or to implement custom workflows that are not supported by z/OSMF's built-in features.

4. Enhanced Functionality: Extend the functionality of z/OSMF. Developers can use the APIs to build new features or services that leverage the capabilities of z/OSMF.

Examples of z/OSMF REST APIs might include APIs to retrieve the status of a workflow, submit a job, fetch job logs, manage software instances, or create an incident report. By offering these APIs, z/OSMF gives organizations the flexibility to manage their z/OS systems in a way that best fits their needs and integrates seamlessly with their existing IT infrastructure and processes.

8. Network Infrastructure in z/OSMF

THE NETWORK INFRASTRUCTURE is an essential part of the z/OS Management Facility (z/OSMF) infrastructure. It establishes the connection between the z/OSMF server, running on IBM's mainframes, and its clients, which can be anywhere with internet access. Let's elaborate on its key components:

1. Routers: These are devices that forward data packets between computer networks. They determine the best path for forwarding the packets to their destination. In z/OSMF, routers play a critical role in connecting the client systems with the mainframe where the server component is hosted.

2. Switches: Network switches are crucial in managing the traffic within an organization's network. They channel incoming data from multiple input ports to the specific output port that will take the data toward its intended destination. In the case of z/OSMF, switches ensure that requests and responses are efficiently exchanged between the server and clients.

3. Firewalls: These devices provide a layer of security for the network. They monitor and control incoming and outgoing network traffic based on predetermined security rules. In the context of z/OSMF, firewalls help protect the mainframe and the z/OSMF server from unauthorized access and potential threats.

4. Load Balancers: In larger implementations, load balancers may be employed to distribute network traffic evenly across multiple servers to ensure no single server becomes overwhelmed with traffic. This results in improved responsiveness and availability of z/OSMF.

5. Network Security: Besides firewalls, network security includes various policies, procedures, and measures to prevent unauthorized access, misuse, malfunction, modification, or denial of network-accessible resources.

6. Network Devices: In addition to the aforementioned components, other devices such as modems, hubs, or repeaters might be part of the network infrastructure, depending on the specific design of the network.

In summary, the network infrastructure plays a pivotal role in the functionality of z/OSMF. It facilitates the communication between the z/OSMF server and clients, ensuring data is correctly routed and delivered in a secure manner. Given the critical nature of tasks managed through z/OSMF, maintaining a robust and secure network infrastructure is essential.

Chapter 4: Installing and Configuring z/OSMF

This chapter will guide you through the process of installing and configuring z/OSMF in your z/OS environment. The installation and configuration process involves several key steps to ensure the correct functioning of z/OSMF. Here are the main sections in this chapter:

4.1 Installation Process: This section provides a step-by-step walkthrough on how to install z/OSMF on a z/OS system. It will cover the necessary prerequisites, the different components you need to install, and how to perform the installation process, including setting up the WebSphere Application Server and deploying the z/OSMF war file.

4.2 Configuration Settings: Once the installation is complete, you will need to configure z/OSMF to suit your specific environment. This section will guide you through the various configuration settings, including setting up network settings, configuring security settings, enabling necessary services, and other important parameters.

4.3 Verifying Installation: After installing and configuring z/OSMF, you'll want to verify that the installation was successful and that z/OSMF is functioning as expected. This section will guide you through the process of checking the installation, including how to troubleshoot common issues that might occur during the installation process.

By the end of this chapter, you should be well equipped to install and configure z/OSMF, ensuring it's set up correctly to manage your z/OS system.

4.1 Installation Process

THE INSTALLATION PROCESS of z/OSMF involves multiple steps and the prerequisite software. It generally involves setting up the required software and services, installing the actual z/OSMF software, and finally setting up the services and features of z/OSMF.

Here's a general outline of the steps involved:

1. Prerequisites: Before installing z/OSMF, you need to ensure that your system meets all the necessary prerequisites. This typically includes having a certain level of the z/OS operating system and having the IBM WebSphere Application Server (WAS) installed.

2. Set up WebSphere Application Server (WAS): The z/OSMF server component is hosted on IBM's WebSphere Application Server. This step involves installing and setting up the WAS if it isn't already installed and configured.

3. Install the z/OSMF Software: Once the prerequisites are met and the WAS is set up, the next step is to install the z/OSMF software. This usually involves transferring the software package to the mainframe system, extracting it, and then running the installation process.

4. Deploy z/OSMF Application: After the z/OSMF software is installed, the next step is to deploy the z/OSMF application on the WAS. This includes setting up the necessary server profiles and resources in WAS and deploying the z/OSMF application.

5. Configure z/OSMF Services: After deploying the z/OSMF application, you will need to configure the z/OSMF services. This involves configuring the system parameters and defining the necessary resources for each z/OSMF service.

6. Start z/OSMF Server: Once everything is installed and configured, the final step in the installation process is to start the z/OSMF server. After the server is started, you should be able to access the z/OSMF web interface from a browser.

Please note that the actual steps can vary depending on the specific version of z/OSMF and the specific configuration of your system. Always refer to the official IBM documentation for the most accurate and detailed installation instructions.

1. Prerequisites for z/OSMF Installation

BEFORE INSTALLING Z/OS Management Facility (z/OSMF), there are certain prerequisites that your system needs to meet. These requirements are critical to ensure the smooth installation and operation of z/OSMF on your z/OS system. Here are the common prerequisites:

1.1 Operating System: z/OSMF runs on the z/OS operating system, so your system needs to have a compatible version of z/OS installed. The required version might vary depending on the version of z/OSMF you are installing. As of my knowledge cut-off in September 2021, z/OS V2.4 or higher was typically required. Please refer to the latest IBM documentation to know the specific version requirements for your desired z/OSMF version.

1.2 IBM WebSphere Application Server (WAS): IBM WebSphere Application Server provides the runtime environment for z/OSMF. You must have a compatible version of WAS installed on your system. Again, the required version might depend on the version of z/OSMF you're installing.

1.3 Java SDK: z/OSMF is a Java-based application, so you need to have a compatible version of the IBM SDK for z/OS Java Technology Edition installed on your system.

1.4 System Resources: You must ensure that your system has sufficient hardware resources to run z/OSMF. This includes CPU, memory, and storage resources.

1.5 Network Access: Your z/OS system needs to be correctly set up to allow network access to z/OSMF. This might involve configuring network settings and firewall rules.

1.6 Security: You should also have a plan for managing security for z/OSMF, including user roles and access permissions.

It's important to note that this is a general overview and the actual prerequisites might vary. Always refer to the latest IBM documentation for the specific prerequisites for your intended version of z/OSMF.

2. Set up WebSphere Application Server (WAS)

WEBSPHERE APPLICATION Server (WAS) is a software framework developed by IBM that provides an environment to deploy and run Java-based web applications, such as z/OSMF. Here are the steps you generally need to follow to set up WAS:

2.1 Install WAS: The first step in setting up WAS is to install the software on your z/OS system. The installation process can vary depending on the version of WAS and the specific configuration of your system, so you should refer to the WAS installation guide provided by IBM for detailed instructions.

2.2 Create WAS Profile: Once WAS is installed, you need to create a WAS profile. The profile contains the runtime environment for your applications and includes settings such as the application server's name, port values, and security settings.

2.3 Configure WAS: After creating the profile, you'll need to configure WAS to suit your requirements. This could include configuring security settings, database connectivity, user directories, and other important parameters.

2.4 Deploy Applications: Once WAS is configured, you can deploy your applications. In the case of z/OSMF, this means deploying the z/OSMF application on WAS.

2.5 Start and Stop WAS: After deploying the applications, you should know how to start and stop the WAS server. You start the server to allow it to accept requests and stop it when you need to shut it down for maintenance or other reasons.

It's important to note that these steps provide a general overview, and the specific steps can vary depending on the version of WAS and the specific configuration of your system. Always refer to the official IBM documentation for the most accurate and detailed instructions.

3. Install the z/OSMF Software

ONCE THE PREREQUISITES are fulfilled and WAS is ready, you can proceed to install the z/OSMF software on your mainframe. The installation of z/OSMF follows a series of steps which might vary slightly based on your system's specific configuration and the z/OSMF version you are installing. However, the general process is as follows:

3.1 Obtain the Software: The first step is to obtain the z/OSMF software package. This can be acquired from IBM's software download portal or via other means provided by IBM. The software is typically delivered as a compressed file.

3.2 Transfer the Software: After obtaining the software, you'll need to transfer the software package to your z/OS system. This can be done using a variety of file transfer methods. The method used may depend on your network setup and the specific policies of your organization.

3.3 Unpack and Install the Software: Once the software is transferred to your z/OS system, you'll need to unpack the software package. This typically involves using a utility to extract the files from the package. After unpacking the software, you can proceed with the installation process. This usually involves running a series of jobs or scripts that install the software onto your system.

3.4 Customize the Installation: Depending on your requirements, you may need to customize the installation. This could involve configuring certain settings, enabling or disabling specific features, or integrating the software with other systems or services.

Please note that this is a general overview of the process, and the actual steps can vary depending on the version of z/OSMF you're installing and the specific configuration of your system. Always refer to the official IBM documentation for the most accurate and detailed installation instructions.

4. Deploy z/OSMF Application

THE DEPLOYMENT OF THE z/OSMF application is a crucial part of the installation process, as it makes the z/OSMF software available for use within the WebSphere Application Server (WAS) environment. Here is a general outline of the process:

4.1 Create WAS Profile for z/OSMF: As a first step, you need to create a new WAS profile specifically for z/OSMF if you haven't done so already. The profile contains the runtime environment for z/OSMF, including configuration details such as the server name, port values, security settings, etc.

4.2 Configure Server Resources: Next, configure the server resources that z/OSMF will need to run effectively. This could include defining the JDBC data sources, J2C authentication aliases, and other necessary resources in WAS.

4.3 Deploy z/OSMF Application: After setting up the profile and configuring server resources, you are ready to deploy the z/OSMF application. The deployment process involves adding the z/OSMF software as an application in WAS. This makes z/OSMF available as a service that can be accessed via the WAS.

4.4 Start the Application: With the z/OSMF application now deployed on WAS, the last step is to start the application. Once started, z/OSMF should be accessible to clients over the network.

This general process should provide an overview of what deploying the z/OSMF application involves. However, always refer to the official IBM documentation for specific instructions tailored to your version of z/OSMF and WAS, and your system's configuration.

5. Configure z/OSMF Services

AFTER DEPLOYING THE z/OSMF application, the next step is to configure the z/OSMF services. This process involves adjusting system parameters and defining the necessary resources that the services will use to perform their tasks. Here's a general outline of the process:

5.1 Define System Parameters: z/OSMF services rely on a set of system parameters to operate effectively. These parameters might include settings related to performance, security, networking, and more. You will need to adjust these settings based on your organization's needs and the specific requirements of your z/OSMF installation.

5.2 Configure z/OSMF Core Services: Each z/OSMF core service (like Workflow Services, Incident Log Services, Software Management Services, etc.) requires its own configuration. This might involve defining settings related to the service's operation, specifying necessary resources, or integrating the service with other systems or services.

5.3 Configure z/OSMF Plugins: If you are using any z/OSMF plugins, you will also need to configure these. Like the core services, plugins may require specific resources or settings in order to operate properly.

5.4 Test Configuration: After configuring the z/OSMF services, it's crucial to test the configuration to ensure that everything works as expected. This could involve running a series of tests or checks to validate the configuration.

Remember, the specifics of this process can vary based on the version of z/OSMF you're using and the specific configuration of your system. Always refer to the official IBM documentation for the most accurate and detailed instructions.

6. Start z/OSMF Server

THE FINAL STEP OF THE installation process is to start the z/OSMF server. After installation and configuration, the z/OSMF application is ready to be put into operation. Here's a high-level overview of this process:

6.1 Start WAS Server: The first step in starting the z/OSMF server is to start the WebSphere Application Server (WAS) that hosts the z/OSMF application. This usually involves running a command from the command line interface of the z/OS system.

6.2 Verify WAS Startup: After starting WAS, you should verify that it has started up correctly. You can usually do this by checking the server logs for any startup errors and ensuring that WAS is now listening for connections on the expected network ports.

6.3 Start z/OSMF Application: Once WAS is running, you can start the z/OSMF application. This is usually done through the WAS administration console, where you can select the z/OSMF application and choose the option to start it.

6.4 Verify z/OSMF Startup: After starting the z/OSMF application, you should verify that it has started up correctly. Like with WAS, this usually involves checking the server logs for any startup errors. You can also try accessing the z/OSMF web interface from a web browser to ensure that it's running and accessible.

This process marks the completion of the z/OSMF installation. You should now have a running z/OSMF server that you can access and start using for your system management tasks. As always, be sure to refer to the official IBM documentation for detailed, step-by-step instructions that are specific to your system configuration and z/OSMF version.

4.2 Configuration Settings

IN THE CONFIGURATION phase of the z/OSMF installation, a number of settings need to be defined and adjusted to match your organization's requirements and the specifications of your system. Here's a high-level overview of some of the primary configuration areas:

1. System Parameters: System parameters dictate how the z/OSMF system will interact with its underlying operating system and hardware. These parameters include settings for memory allocation, processor usage, input/output settings, and more.

2. Network Configuration: Network settings determine how z/OSMF communicates over the network. These settings could include the server's IP address and port number, firewall settings, proxy settings, and more.

3. Security Settings: Security settings are essential to protect your z/OSMF installation and its data. This could involve configuring user roles and permissions, setting up secure connections (such as SSL/TLS), configuring authentication methods, etc.

4. Service Configuration: Each of the z/OSMF services will likely require its own specific configuration. This might involve defining resources for the service, setting up connections to other systems or services, defining operational parameters, and so on.

5. Plugin Configuration: If you are using any z/OSMF plugins, these will also need to be configured. This could involve specifying resources for the plugin, integrating it with other services, or setting up any necessary parameters for its operation.

Please note that the specifics of these settings can vary depending on your specific use case, system setup, and the version of z/OSMF you're using. For detailed instructions, always refer to the official IBM documentation or reach out to IBM support.

1. System Parameters

WHEN INSTALLING AND configuring z/OSMF, a number of system parameters need to be set according to the organization's requirements and the specific hardware configuration of the system. This is a high-level overview of the main categories of system parameters:

1. Memory Allocation: The memory allocation parameter is used to specify how much system memory should be allocated to z/OSMF. This is important because it can significantly impact the performance of z/OSMF. For example, if too little memory is allocated, z/OSMF may run slowly or experience out-of-memory errors.

2. Processor Usage: Processor usage parameters determine how the system's CPU resources are distributed among z/OSMF and other applications running on the system. These settings can help ensure that z/OSMF has enough CPU resources to function efficiently, without unnecessarily consuming resources that other applications need.

3. Input/Output Settings: These settings control how z/OSMF interacts with the system's input and output devices, such as terminals, printers, and disk drives. For instance, it may be necessary to configure the settings for the devices that z/OSMF will use for logging, data storage, and user interface.

4. System Resource Settings: These parameters control how z/OSMF interacts with various system resources. For example, you might need to specify the directories where z/OSMF can find certain system libraries or the ports that z/OSMF should use for network communications.

5. Performance Settings: Performance settings control how z/OSMF optimizes its operations. These could include parameters for task scheduling, process prioritization, and other aspects of system performance.

Note: The exact parameters and their configuration will depend on your specific system setup and the version of z/OSMF you are installing. Always refer to the official IBM documentation for specific instructions and recommendations.

2. Network Configuration

Z/OSMF IS DESIGNED to be accessed remotely via a network, typically a TCP/IP network. This means that during installation and configuration, you will need to set up several network parameters to ensure proper communication. These parameters could include the following:

1. IP Address and Port Number: Each z/OSMF server must be assigned a unique IP address and port number to enable other devices on the network to establish a connection to it. This address and port number will be used by the client devices to access the z/OSMF interface.

2. Firewall Settings: If your z/OSMF server is protected by a firewall, you will need to configure the firewall to allow incoming and outgoing traffic on the server's IP address and port number. This may involve opening specific ports on the firewall and setting rules for the type of traffic that can pass through.

3. Proxy Settings: If your organization uses a proxy server to manage internet traffic, you may need to configure z/OSMF to connect to the internet through this proxy. This can involve setting the proxy's IP address and port number, as well as any necessary authentication information.

4. Network Protocols: Depending on your network's configuration, you may need to set parameters related to the network protocols used by z/OSMF. For example, you may need to enable or disable specific protocols, or set parameters for how these protocols should function.

5. Security Settings: Network security settings might include enabling SSL/TLS for secure communication, setting up certificates, and configuring encryption settings.

6. Bandwidth Management: Depending on the network traffic and load, you may need to manage bandwidth to ensure that z/OSMF does not consume more than its fair share of network resources.

Please note that the specifics of these settings can vary depending on your specific network setup and the version of z/OSMF you're using. For detailed instructions, always refer to the official IBM documentation or reach out to IBM support.

3. Security Settings

ENSURING THE SECURITY of your z/OSMF installation is crucial to protect your system's data and maintain the integrity of your operations. Here are some of the security settings you might need to configure during the installation of z/OSMF:

1. User Roles and Permissions: z/OSMF allows you to define various roles, each with its own set of permissions. These roles determine what operations a user can perform in the system. For instance, an administrator might have full access to all functions, while a regular user might only have access to a subset of functions.

2. Secure Connections (SSL/TLS): Secure Sockets Layer (SSL) and Transport Layer Security (TLS) are protocols for establishing secure connections over a network. Enabling SSL or TLS for z/OSMF ensures that all data transmitted between the client and server is encrypted and secure from eavesdropping.

3. Authentication Methods: Authentication settings determine how users will prove their identity when logging into z/OSMF. This could be through a username/password combination, digital certificates, or other methods.

4. Firewall Settings: As part of the security setup, you might need to configure the firewall settings to protect the z/OSMF server from unauthorized access. This could involve setting rules about who can access the server and what types of activities are allowed.

5. Audit Logs: Enabling audit logs ensures that all activities performed within z/OSMF are logged. These logs can be reviewed to identify any suspicious activities and can serve as an important tool for incident response and forensics.

6. Data Protection: This involves setting up protections for the data stored by z/OSMF. This might include configuring backups, setting up encryption for data at rest, and other similar measures.

As always, the specifics of these settings will depend on your organization's security requirements and policies, as well as the version of z/OSMF you're using. Always refer to the official IBM documentation or consult with a security professional when setting up these configurations.

4. Service Configuration

SERVICE CONFIGURATION in z/OSMF is crucial to ensure each service operates correctly and efficiently. Each service within z/OSMF has its unique requirements and, as such, will require specific configurations. Here are examples of what you might need to set up:

1. Defining Resources: Each service may need to interact with certain resources in the z/OS system, such as databases, directories, or other services. During configuration, you'll define these resources and the access permissions each service has.

2. Setting Up Connections: Services within z/OSMF may need to interact with other systems or services. This could involve configuring network connections, setting up secure data transmission, or specifying interaction protocols.

3. Operational Parameters: Each service will have operational parameters that define how it performs its tasks. These could include settings for how often a service performs certain operations, how it handles errors, or what conditions trigger certain actions.

4. Workflow Services: For workflow services, you might need to define standard workflows or templates. These can be used repeatedly and modified as needed.

5. Security Settings: Each service may also have its security settings, including access controls and data encryption options.

6. Logging and Reporting Settings: Services may also have settings for how they log their activities or report their status. These settings can be crucial for monitoring service performance and troubleshooting issues.

As with other parts of z/OSMF setup, the specifics of service configuration will depend on your specific needs and the version of z/OSMF you are using. Always refer to the official IBM documentation for the most accurate and up-to-date information.

5. Plugin Configuration

PLUGINS IN Z/OSMF PROVIDE additional functionality and features beyond the core services. They can be developed by IBM, third-party vendors, or developed internally within your organization. Each plugin will have its configuration requirements, and here's what you might typically need to do:

1. Specifying Resources: Similar to core services, plugins may also require specific resources to function correctly. These could be databases, network connections, or specific system files or directories. You'll need to define these resources and set appropriate access permissions.

2. Plugin Integration: Some plugins may need to integrate with other services or plugins within z/OSMF. This could involve setting up communication channels, defining data formats for exchange, or specifying protocols for interaction.

3. Operational Parameters: Plugins will have operational parameters that govern their functionality. These could include settings for how the plugin operates, when it operates, or what conditions trigger certain actions.

4. Security Settings: Depending on the function of the plugin, it may also have its security settings. This could include data encryption options, user access controls, or settings for secure data transmission.

5. Logging and Reporting Settings: Plugins may also have settings for how they log their activities or report their status. This can be crucial for tracking plugin performance, monitoring its health, and diagnosing any issues.

Remember that the specific requirements for each plugin will depend on the plugin's purpose and design. Always refer to the plugin's documentation for specific instructions on how to configure it correctly.

Please note that plugins should be chosen carefully, as they can impact the overall performance and security of your z/OSMF system. Always ensure that any plugins you use are from a trusted source and have been thoroughly tested for compatibility with your specific system setup.

4.3 Verifying Installation

AFTER THE INSTALLATION and configuration of z/OSMF, it's critical to ensure everything is correctly set up and functioning as expected. Here are the typical steps you'd take to verify your z/OSMF installation:

1. Start the z/OSMF Server: The first step in verifying your z/OSMF installation is to start the z/OSMF server. If the server starts up without any errors, it's a good sign that the installation was successful.
2. Access the z/OSMF Web Interface: After the server is up, try accessing the z/OSMF web interface through a web browser. The web interface is the primary means of interacting with z/OSMF, and being able to access it indicates that the server and network configuration are correct.
3. Log In: Try logging into z/OSMF using a user account. Successful login demonstrates that the security settings are correctly configured and user authentication is working as expected.
4. Test Core Services: Perform some basic operations with the core z/OSMF services. This could involve creating a simple workflow, viewing a system log, or installing a software package. Successful operation of these services shows that they're correctly set up.
5. Test Plugins: If you've installed any z/OSMF plugins, you should also test these to ensure they're working correctly. Depending on the plugin, this could involve performing specific tasks or checking certain functions.
6. Review System Logs: Lastly, review the z/OSMF system logs to check for any errors or warnings that might have occurred during the installation or during the testing process. Addressing any issues at this stage can prevent problems later on.

Remember that a successful verification process doesn't just mean that the z/OSMF system is correctly installed; it also means that it's ready to be used in a production environment. Therefore, it's essential to take this process seriously and ensure everything is functioning as expected.

1. Start the z/OSMF Server

STARTING THE Z/OSMF server is a crucial step to verify the successful installation of z/OSMF. To start the server, you typically execute a specific command in the operating system console or via a system management interface.

Once the command is issued, the server starts by loading the necessary components, services, and plugins. It initializes its runtime environment, starts the services, and then awaits incoming connections from clients.

During the startup process, the system performs numerous checks. It validates the system configuration, ensures that all necessary resources are available, and checks the integrity of the system files. If there are any issues, such as configuration errors or missing resources, the system typically logs these problems and might even halt the startup process.

If the server starts up without any errors, it generally means that the z/OSMF system files are intact, the configuration is correct, and all necessary resources are available. It signifies that the server is ready to accept client connections and perform its management tasks.

It's recommended to carefully review the server startup logs, even if no errors are apparent during the startup process. The logs may contain warnings or other information that could indicate potential issues. These issues might not prevent the server from starting, but they could affect system performance or stability.

In conclusion, being able to start the z/OSMF server is a positive sign that the system is correctly installed and configured, and it's a vital step in verifying the z/OSMF installation.

2. Access the z/OSMF Web Interface

ACCESSING THE Z/OSMF web interface is a significant aspect of verifying your z/OSMF installation. The z/OSMF web interface is a graphical user interface (GUI) that enables administrators to manage and interact with z/OS systems in a convenient and user-friendly way. This web-based GUI is hosted on the z/OSMF server and accessed through a web browser.

To access the z/OSMF web interface, you typically open a web browser and enter the URL for the z/OSMF server. The URL typically includes the server's IP address or hostname and the port number on which z/OSMF is listening.

After entering the URL, the browser sends a request to the z/OSMF server. The server processes the request and sends back a response, which should be the login page of the z/OSMF web interface.

If you can reach this page, it means that the z/OSMF server is running, the network configuration is correct, and the server is accessible over the network. You should see a login prompt where you can enter your user credentials.

After successfully logging in, you should be able to navigate the interface and access the various features and services of z/OSMF. If all these steps are successful, it's a good indication that z/OSMF is installed correctly and functioning as expected.

Remember to also check that all pages load correctly and that there are no errors or missing elements. This will help confirm that the web application files are properly installed and that the server is correctly rendering the web interface.

In summary, being able to access and navigate the z/OSMF web interface is an essential step in verifying your z/OSMF installation. It shows that the server, network, and web application are correctly configured and functioning as expected.

3. Log In

LOGGING INTO Z/OSMF is another crucial step in verifying the installation. It primarily tests two things: the user authentication system and the application's security settings. Here's a more detailed look at what happens during this process:

1. User Authentication: When you enter your username and password and click 'log in', the z/OSMF application takes your credentials and verifies them against its internal user database or an external authentication service, depending on how it's been configured. If your credentials are correct, the system will authenticate you and allow you to access the application. If the credentials are wrong, the system will deny access. Being able to log in successfully means that the user authentication system is functioning correctly.
2. Access Control: Once you are authenticated and logged in, you should be able to access the various features and services of z/OSMF based on your user role and permissions. For example, if your user account has administrator privileges, you should be able to access all features and services. If your account has more limited permissions, you may only be able to access certain areas of the application. This shows that the system's access control mechanisms are working as expected.

In addition, successful login also demonstrates the correct configuration of session management. Once logged in, the application should maintain your 'logged in' state as you navigate through the application, allowing you to access features and services without needing to re-enter your credentials. This shows that the application's session management system is functioning correctly.

So, being able to log in successfully to z/OSMF verifies that the application's user authentication, access control, and session management systems are correctly configured and functioning as expected. It confirms that the application's security settings are appropriate and that users can securely access and use the system.

4. Test Core Services

TESTING THE CORE SERVICES is a critical step in validating your z/OSMF installation. Here's how you can verify the functioning of these services:

1. Workflow Services: Start by creating a simple workflow. A workflow in z/OSMF is a defined sequence of steps designed to automate a complex task. You could create a workflow that performs a basic system check or a similar operation. If you can create, start, and complete the workflow without any errors, it's an indication that the workflow services are functioning correctly.
2. Incident Log Services: Try accessing the incident log through the z/OSMF interface. The incident log records events that occur within the system, such as errors or system failures. If you can view the incident log and it appears to be correctly recording events, it indicates that the incident log services are operational.
3. Software Management Services: Attempt to install a small software package using the software management services. The package could be a simple utility or application. If you can successfully install the software package and it operates as expected, it suggests that the software management services are working correctly.

Note: Before attempting to install any software, be sure to verify that the software is compatible with your system and won't disrupt any critical services.

1. Resource Monitoring Services: Check the system resource usage through the resource monitoring services. This could

involve checking the CPU usage, memory usage, or disk space usage. If the resource monitoring services are providing accurate and timely data, it means they are functioning correctly.

Remember, the core services are crucial for z/OSMF operations. So, it's essential to thoroughly test these services to ensure they're correctly set up and working as expected. This will give you the confidence that your z/OSMF installation is successful and ready to be used for managing your z/OS system.

5. Test Plugins

TESTING YOUR Z/OSMF plugins is a crucial step in ensuring the overall functionality of your z/OS Management Facility. Given that plugins provide additional functionalities to your z/OSMF, it's important to verify their proper operation after installation. Here's how you can verify your plugins:

1. Start the Plugin: The initial step is to make sure the plugin can be started without any errors. If the plugin starts successfully, it suggests that it has been installed correctly and is compatible with your version of z/OSMF.
2. Access Plugin Functions: Access the features or functions provided by the plugin. This could involve performing specific tasks or accessing certain services or resources. Successful operation indicates that the plugin is correctly integrated with z/OSMF and its services.
3. Run Plugin-Specific Tests: Depending on the nature of the plugin, there might be specific tests you can run to verify its functionality. For instance, if you've installed a network configuration plugin, you could attempt to modify a network setting and verify the change.
4. Check Plugin Logs: If the plugin generates logs, check these to see if there are any warnings or errors. Clear logs indicate the plugin is operating without issues.
5. Performance and Stability: Check the performance and stability of the plugin. Ensure it does not cause any disruption to the operation of z/OSMF or impact the performance of other services.

Remember, the plugins are designed to enhance the capabilities of your z/OS Management Facility. Ensuring their proper operation not only verifies your installation process but also confirms that your system is equipped with the enhanced features you require.

6. Review System Logs

SYSTEM LOGS ARE A VITAL tool in any computing environment, and z/OSMF is no exception. They offer a detailed chronological record of events and transactions that have occurred within a system. This log data can be invaluable when troubleshooting problems, identifying security incidents, or ensuring compliance with policies. Here's how you can use system logs to verify your z/OSMF installation:

1. Locate the Logs: The first step is knowing where your system logs are located. In a z/OSMF environment, this could be in the z/OS system log (SYSLOG), the WebSphere Application Server log, the z/OSMF server logs, or other logs depending on your setup.
2. Scan for Errors and Warnings: Review these logs and scan for any messages marked as errors or warnings. These could indicate problems that occurred during the installation process or while testing your z/OSMF environment.
3. Identify Issues: Any error or warning messages should be investigated. They could point to issues with hardware or software configurations, network settings, resource allocation, security permissions, or other aspects of your system.
4. Address Identified Issues: After identifying potential issues, appropriate action should be taken to resolve them. This may involve adjusting configuration settings, fixing installation issues, or troubleshooting hardware or network problems.
5. Monitor Logs Over Time: Don't stop at a single review. Continuous log monitoring is a good practice to promptly detect and address new issues that may arise. There are even automated tools available that can help with this task by alerting you to potential problems as soon as they appear in

your logs.

By thoroughly reviewing your system logs, you can gain confidence that your z/OSMF installation is not only successful but also free from underlying issues that might cause problems in the future. System logs serve as an early warning system, providing insights into what's happening beneath the surface of your computing environment.

Chapter 5: Navigating the z/OSMF Interface

The z/OS Management Facility (z/OSMF) provides a web-based interface that makes it easier for system administrators and operators to manage their z/OS systems. With a user-friendly and intuitive interface, z/OSMF helps streamline and simplify a wide range of management tasks. In this chapter, we will explore the various components of the z/OSMF interface and how to interact with them.

5.1 z/OSMF Dashboard: The z/OSMF Dashboard is the first thing you see when you log into z/OSMF. It serves as the central hub from where you can navigate to various parts of the z/OSMF interface. We will delve into the details of what the dashboard contains and how to navigate it.

5.2 Understanding Panels and Dialogs: Panels and dialogs form the primary components of the z/OSMF interface. Understanding these elements will help you interact with the system efficiently. We'll discuss what they are, how they are structured, and what type of information and interaction they facilitate.

5.3 Keyboard and Mouse Operations: Even though z/OSMF provides a graphical interface, knowing the keyboard and mouse operations can help increase your efficiency. In this section, we will explain the common operations and how to use them for navigation, selection, and other tasks.

By the end of this chapter, you should be familiar with the z/OSMF interface and be able to navigate it comfortably, making your z/OS management tasks more straightforward and efficient.

5.1 z/OSMF Dashboard

THE Z/OSMF DASHBOARD is the central hub of the z/OS Management Facility, presenting users with a clear, organized overview of the system's status and available tasks. The interface is designed to be intuitive and user-friendly, allowing even newcomers to mainframe systems to easily navigate and manage their tasks.

Here are some of the key components of the z/OSMF Dashboard:

1. Navigation Pane: The left side of the dashboard displays a collapsible navigation pane, which contains a list of all available z/OSMF applications and services. You can click on these to access the corresponding features.
2. Workspace Area: The majority of the dashboard is occupied by the workspace area, where the specific panels, tables, or dialogs related to the selected application or service are displayed. The content of this area changes depending on what's selected in the navigation pane.
3. Tasks: Tasks are specific actions or operations that you can initiate from the dashboard. For example, tasks can include creating a new workflow, viewing system logs, or managing installed software. The available tasks change based on the current context.
4. Status Indicators: The dashboard can also display status indicators that provide at-a-glance information about the system's status. For example, it might show indicators for system health, resource utilization, or the status of ongoing tasks.
5. Quick Links: For commonly accessed features or settings, quick links might be provided for easy access. These could include links to certain management tasks, system settings, or help resources.

Overall, the z/OSMF Dashboard is designed to provide easy access to all z/OSMF features and provide a centralized view of the system's status, making it easier for administrators to manage their z/OS systems.

1. Navigation Pane

THE NAVIGATION PANE in the z/OSMF Dashboard is an integral part of the interface, as it provides users with a clear, organized directory of all the available applications, services, and tools. Here's an elaboration on its primary features and functionalities:

Collapsible Categories: The Navigation Pane is organized into collapsible categories, each representing a different aspect of z/OSMF, such as 'Workflows', 'Software Management', 'Incident Log', 'Resource Monitoring', and so on. Clicking on a category expands it to display the associated services or functions.

Quick Access: The Navigation Pane allows users to quickly navigate between different parts of z/OSMF. By simply clicking on a service or application in the Navigation Pane, the corresponding interface is loaded in the Workspace Area. This allows users to switch context quickly, enhancing the efficiency of their management tasks.

Hierarchical Layout: The services and applications in the Navigation Pane are organized hierarchically, with related functions grouped under the same category. This structure not only facilitates quick navigation but also provides users with a clear understanding of how different services and functions are related.

Search Function: In larger systems, the Navigation Pane may contain many different categories and services. A search function allows users to quickly find the service they need without having to manually locate it in the navigation hierarchy.

Customizability: Depending on the specific implementation of z/OSMF, the Navigation Pane may be customizable. Administrators could potentially add, remove, or rearrange categories and services based on their specific needs, providing a tailored management experience.

Overall, the Navigation Pane is a central feature of the z/OSMF Dashboard, providing an organized, easily navigable directory of the system's many management features.

2. Workspace Area

THE WORKSPACE AREA in the z/OSMF Dashboard serves as the main interactive section where users perform various management tasks and operations. Here are some more details about its functionalities:

Dynamic Content Display: The Workspace Area changes dynamically based on what is selected in the Navigation Pane. For instance, if a user clicks on 'Workflows' in the Navigation Pane, the Workspace Area will then display the Workflow management interface. If 'Incident Log' is selected, the incident log viewing and management interface will be displayed instead.

Interactive Panels, Tables, and Dialogs: The Workspace Area houses the interactive elements such as panels, tables, and dialogs, related to the selected application or service. For example, if the Software Management service is selected, the Workspace Area might display a table of installed software, with panels or dialogs for installing new software, updating existing software, or managing software dependencies.

Task Execution: Users carry out their tasks in the Workspace Area. Depending on the service in use, users may fill out forms, make selections, enter commands, or interact with the system in other ways within this area.

Information Display: Besides providing interactive elements for task execution, the Workspace Area also serves to display information back to the user. This could include tables of data, system statuses, logs, task results, and more.

Multi-tab Interface: Depending on the specific implementation of z/OSMF, the Workspace Area may support a multi-tab interface, allowing users to have multiple services or applications open at the same time in different tabs, thereby enhancing multitasking and efficiency.

In essence, the Workspace Area is the 'workhorse' of the z/OSMF Dashboard. It's where users perform their tasks, view system information, and interact with the various z/OSMF services.

3. Tasks

THE TASKS FEATURE IN the z/OSMF dashboard provides users with the ability to initiate specific actions or operations based on their current selection or context. Here's more on what tasks can do in z/OSMF:

Context-Based Operations: The Tasks feature adjusts to the context of the current workspace area. For instance, if a user is in the workflow management interface, the tasks available might be to create a new workflow, edit an existing one, run a workflow, or delete one. If the user switches to the software management interface, the tasks could change to actions such as installing new software, updating software, or managing software dependencies.

Initiating Procedures: Tasks often serve as the starting point for procedures, initiating a series of steps or a process that might involve several screens or panels. For instance, creating a new workflow might open a dialog for naming and defining the workflow, then a sequence of screens for adding, arranging, and configuring tasks in the workflow.

Shortcut for Common Operations: Often, frequently performed or important operations are available directly as tasks. This provides a convenient shortcut for users, allowing them to perform these operations directly from the dashboard without having to navigate through menus or interfaces.

Integration with Other Services: Tasks can also provide integration with other z/OSMF services or even external systems. For example, a task could initiate a process that involves both the workflow service and the software management service, or it could trigger an operation in an external system.

In a nutshell, Tasks are a central aspect of the z/OSMF user interface, providing an intuitive and convenient way for users to initiate actions and operations in the system.

4. Status Indicators

STATUS INDICATORS ARE a crucial part of the z/OSMF dashboard, providing users with an easy way to monitor key system parameters at a glance. Here's a more detailed look at these indicators:

System Health Indicators: These indicators can display the overall health of the z/OSMF system or specific components of the system. For example, they might show whether the z/OSMF server is up and running, whether any critical errors have been reported, or whether all core services are functioning correctly. This allows administrators to quickly spot any major problems with the system.

Resource Utilization Indicators: These indicators show the current usage of system resources. They might display metrics such as CPU usage, memory utilization, disk space usage, network bandwidth usage, and more. Monitoring these indicators can help administrators ensure that the system is performing optimally and that resources are not being over-utilized or under-utilized.

Task Status Indicators: If any tasks are running in the background, the dashboard can display indicators for these tasks. These indicators might show whether the tasks are running, paused, completed, or failed. They might also provide progress updates for ongoing tasks.

Alert Indicators: In case of system issues or problems, alert indicators are displayed to draw attention. They can be color-coded (like red for critical issues or yellow for warnings) and can be associated with system events like service disruptions, security incidents, or performance issues.

Custom Indicators: Depending on the specific setup and requirements of an organization, the dashboard can be configured to display additional custom indicators. These could be related to business-specific metrics, compliance requirements, or other relevant parameters.

In summary, status indicators are an essential part of the z/OSMF dashboard, providing real-time, visual feedback about the system's status and helping administrators monitor and manage the system more effectively.

5. Quick Links

QUICK LINKS ARE A CRUCIAL part of the z/OSMF Dashboard interface, designed to enhance user experience by providing easy, one-click access to commonly used features, tasks, settings, or resources. These shortcuts can be critical for efficiency, especially for system administrators who need to quickly navigate through the system and perform routine tasks.

Here's a deeper dive into Quick Links:

Common Management Tasks: Some Quick Links may lead directly to interfaces for commonly performed management tasks. For example, creating a new workflow, monitoring system resources, viewing active tasks, or accessing incident logs.

System Settings: Quick Links might also provide direct access to frequently modified system settings. For example, adjusting resource allocations, updating security configurations, or changing network settings.

Help Resources: For immediate assistance, Quick Links may point to help resources such as user manuals, troubleshooting guides, community forums, or direct contact to support. This aids in quickly finding solutions to problems or getting clarification on functionality.

Frequently Used Services or Plugins: If there are services or plugins that a user often interacts with, Quick Links can directly lead to these sections, reducing navigation time.

User-Specific Links: Depending on the user's role and permissions, certain Quick Links might be available to some users but not others. For example, an administrator might have Quick Links to system-wide configurations, while a regular user might have Quick Links to his/her own tasks or settings.

Quick Links are customizable depending on the specific needs and usage patterns of an organization or individual users. This feature greatly enhances usability and productivity, allowing users to navigate the z/OSMF system more swiftly and smoothly.

5.2 Understanding Panels and Dialogs

THE Z/OSMF INTERFACE makes use of panels and dialogs to display information and interact with users. Understanding how these elements work is critical to effectively using the z/OSMF system.

1. Panels: Panels are areas within the workspace that display content related to a specific task, service, or function. For example, you might have a panel displaying the status of all running jobs, another panel showing system resource usage, or another panel where you can create and manage workflows. Panels can be customized and arranged based on user preferences or the tasks at hand.
2. Dialogs: Dialogs are pop-up windows that are used to gather input from the user or display important information. For example, when creating a new workflow, a dialog might appear asking for the details of the workflow. Similarly, if there's a system error, a dialog might pop up to inform the user about the issue.

The specific panels and dialogs that a user interacts with will depend on the tasks they're performing and the services they're using. However, understanding these basic interface elements and how they work will help users navigate the z/OSMF system more effectively.

1. Panels

PANELS IN THE Z/OSMF interface act as the primary interaction point for the user with the system. They are essentially containers that display content and controls related to specific tasks, services, or functions within z/OSMF. The content within a panel can vary widely based on its purpose. For instance:

- Job Monitoring Panel: A panel could display information about all running jobs on the z/OS system. This could include details such as job ID, owner, status (running, completed, failed, etc.), CPU usage, start and end times, and so on.
- Resource Usage Panel: Another panel might provide real-time statistics about system resource usage. This could include data about CPU utilization, memory usage, disk I/O, network bandwidth, and so on. It might present this information in various forms, such as tables, charts, or graphs.
- Workflow Management Panel: Yet another panel might provide controls for creating, managing, and executing workflows. It could allow you to define new workflows, specify the steps and conditions within a workflow, start and stop workflows, and monitor their progress.

A significant advantage of using panels is their customizability. The z/OSMF interface is usually configurable, allowing each user to arrange panels on their dashboard according to their preferences or needs. For example, a system administrator who frequently monitors system performance might place the Resource Usage Panel in a prominent location on their dashboard, while a developer who regularly creates and manages workflows might prioritize the Workflow Management Panel.

Additionally, some panels might allow for further customization within them, such as specifying which columns to display in a table or how to format data. This level of customizability helps users create a working environment that best suits their specific roles and tasks.

2. Dialogs

DIALOGS IN THE Z/OSMF interface are interactive elements that are used to present detailed information, prompts, warnings, or errors to the user. They also serve as a mechanism to gather specific inputs or confirmations from the user. Here's how dialogs may be used in the z/OSMF environment:

- Input Dialogs: These types of dialogs are used when z/OSMF needs specific information from the user to perform a task. For example, if a user wants to create a new workflow, an input dialog might appear asking for details such as the workflow's name, description, and steps. The user can enter the required information into the dialog, and upon confirmation, z/OSMF can use this information to create the workflow.
- Confirmation Dialogs: Confirmation dialogs are used to make sure that the user wants to proceed with an action that could have significant effects. For example, if a user attempts to delete a workflow, a confirmation dialog might appear asking the user to confirm that they indeed want to delete the workflow. This helps prevent accidental deletions or changes.
- Information Dialogs: These dialogs are used to provide the user with important information or updates. For example, if a system task has completed successfully, an information dialog might appear to inform the user of the success. Alternatively, if a task has failed, the dialog might provide information about the error and possible troubleshooting steps.
- Error Dialogs: These types of dialogs are used to display error messages to the user. If there's a system error or if a task fails, an error dialog might pop up to inform the user about the issue. The dialog may provide detailed error messages that can

help in diagnosing and resolving the problem.

Dialogs in z/OSMF are designed to be straightforward and intuitive, ensuring that users can quickly understand and respond to the information or prompts. They can be closed once the user has finished interacting with them. This allows for an efficient, user-friendly experience when using z/OSMF.

5.3 Keyboard and Mouse Operations

THE Z/OS MANAGEMENT Facility (z/OSMF) user interface, like many modern web-based interfaces, supports a variety of keyboard and mouse operations to interact with the system. These operations allow users to effectively navigate through the z/OSMF interface, perform tasks, and manage system resources. Here is a breakdown of some of these operations:

1. Mouse Operations:
   - Clicking: Clicking on various elements of the user interface is the most basic mouse operation. You can click to select options, open dialog boxes, launch applications, and submit forms.
   - Right-Clicking: In some contexts, right-clicking might open context menus with additional options related to the item you're clicking on.
   - Double-Clicking: Double-clicking might be used to open certain items, similar to how you might double-click a file or folder in a desktop environment.
   - Dragging and Dropping: Dragging and dropping might be used in some contexts, for example, to rearrange elements on the dashboard, or to add items to a workflow.
2. Keyboard Operations:
   - Typing: Typing is used for entering text in input fields, such as when configuring settings or entering data.
   - Tabbing: The Tab key can be used to move the focus between different elements of the user interface, such as input fields, buttons, and menus. This can be

especially useful for keyboard-focused navigation.
  - Shortcut Keys: Certain actions may have keyboard shortcuts associated with them, allowing you to perform these actions more quickly. These will depend on the specific context and the design of the z/OSMF interface.
  - Enter Key: The Enter key can often be used to submit forms or confirm dialog boxes.
  - Arrow Keys: Arrow keys can be used to navigate within certain elements, such as menus or lists.

These are general principles and the specific operations available may vary based on the context within z/OSMF, the specific tasks being performed, and the configuration of the z/OSMF interface. Always refer to the user guide or help documentation for the specific operations and shortcuts available in your environment.

Chapter 6: Using z/OSMF for System Management

Chapter 6 of this guide dives into the practical use of z/OSMF for System Management, elaborating on how administrators can leverage this powerful framework for efficient and effective system management. The chapter details the usage of z/OSMF for various tasks such as Incident Log Management, Workflow Management, and Configuration Assistance.

- 6.1 Incident Log Management: This subsection describes how administrators can use z/OSMF to manage incident logs. z/OSMF provides an Incident Log service that allows administrators to view, categorize, track, and manage system incidents, assisting in efficient problem determination and system recovery.
- 6.2 Workflow Management: Workflow Management is an essential part of system administration, enabling the automation of complex, multi-step tasks. This subsection details how workflows can be created, monitored, and managed within z/OSMF, significantly increasing efficiency and reducing the possibility of human error.
- 6.3 Configuration Assistant: Configuring various z/OS components can be a complex task. This subsection highlights how z/OSMF simplifies this process by providing a unified interface for managing system settings. Configuration Assistant services guide administrators through configuration tasks and help to ensure consistency across the system.

6.1 Incident Log Management:

Z/OSMF'S INCIDENT LOG Management service provides a comprehensive solution for dealing with system incidents. This involves maintaining a record of all incidents that occur within the system, providing necessary tools to analyze these incidents, and keeping track of incident resolution processes. Here's a deeper look into what this involves:

1. Incident Recording: When a system incident occurs, it gets logged in the incident log. This log includes details about the incident such as the time it occurred, the system or service it affected, any error messages or codes associated with it, and potentially some information about what the system was doing when the incident occurred.
2. Incident Analysis: Using the data recorded in the incident log, z/OSMF provides tools to analyze the cause of the incident. This could involve looking at patterns of incidents, examining system data from around the time of the incident, or using debugging tools to further investigate the problem.
3. Incident Tracking: The incident log management service also provides features for tracking the progress of resolving incidents. This can involve assigning incidents to particular administrators, setting priority levels for incidents, and recording notes about the steps taken to resolve the incident.
4. Incident Resolution: Once the cause of an incident has been identified, the incident log management service can also help administrators to resolve the incident. This could involve providing tools to fix the issue, offering suggestions for solutions, or directing administrators to relevant resources or documentation.
5. Reporting: Finally, the incident log management service

provides reporting features, which allow administrators to generate reports about incidents. These reports can be used to inform other stakeholders, analyze the overall health and stability of the system, and plan for future system improvements or changes.

1. Incident Recording

IN THE CONTEXT OF Z/OSMF, Incident Recording is a crucial part of Incident Log Management. It functions as the initial step in problem resolution and involves automatically recording any aberrations, errors, or faults that occur within the system.

The process of incident recording includes the following:

1. Detection: The z/OSMF system continually monitors all system operations and processes. In the event of a fault, anomaly, or error, it is detected and flagged for recording.
2. Logging: Once an incident is detected, it's recorded in the incident log. The recording process captures a wide range of details, which can vary depending on the nature of the incident, but typically includes:
    - Timestamp: The exact date and time when the incident occurred.
    - Incident ID: A unique identifier assigned to each incident for easy tracking and referencing.
    - System or Service Affected: Information about which part of the system or which service was affected or involved in the incident.
    - Error Messages/Codes: Any error messages or codes that were generated as part of the incident.
    - Status: The current status of the incident, such as whether it's unresolved, under investigation, or resolved.
    - Additional Context: This can include any additional data or context about what the system or the affected service was doing when the incident occurred. This might involve log entries from other system components, data values, or state

information.

3. Categorization: Incidents might be automatically categorized based on their type or severity, which can assist in prioritizing and handling the incidents later.
4. Notification: Depending on the system settings, incident recording might also trigger notifications to be sent to administrators or other relevant parties, informing them of the incident.

Remember that the main goal of incident recording is to capture a comprehensive snapshot of the situation when an incident occurs, providing a starting point for subsequent investigation and resolution efforts.

2. Incident Analysis

INCIDENT ANALYSIS IS a vital aspect of Incident Log Management within z/OSMF, aiding in the identification of the root cause of system issues and providing valuable insights to prevent their recurrence.

Here's an expounded explanation of the different aspects of Incident Analysis:

1. Incident Overview: The first step in incident analysis typically involves reviewing the incidents recorded in the log, understanding the reported error messages or codes, and getting an overview of what happened.
2. Pattern Analysis: Analyzing patterns and trends in incidents can often reveal important insights. For example, if a certain type of incident tends to occur at specific times or under certain conditions, this might suggest a particular cause or trigger. Pattern analysis could involve looking at the frequency, timing, and distribution of incidents, as well as correlations between different types of incidents.
3. System Data Examination: The data recorded about the system state at the time of the incident can be crucial in understanding its cause. This might involve examining log entries from other system components, looking at the values of specific data items, or reviewing the status and configuration of the system or services involved in the incident.
4. Debugging Tools: For more in-depth analysis, z/OSMF provides a range of debugging tools. These tools can be used to dig deeper into the system's behavior, such as stepping through the execution of a service, inspecting the values of variables, or examining the system's memory or storage. These

tools can be especially helpful for complex incidents where the cause isn't immediately apparent from the incident log or system data.

5. Reporting and Documentation: Finally, the findings of the incident analysis are typically documented in a report, which can then be used to inform decision-making, drive improvements, and support communication with stakeholders. z/OSMF can generate various reports based on the incident analysis, providing a structured and organized view of the incident and the subsequent investigation.

It's worth noting that incident analysis often requires a deep understanding of the system and its components, as well as a systematic approach to investigating and solving problems. The specific steps and tools used can vary depending on the nature of the incident and the specific characteristics of the system.

3. Incident Tracking

INCIDENT TRACKING WITHIN z/OSMF ensures a structured, organized, and efficient response to system incidents. This involves the following aspects:

1. Incident Assignment: Incidents can be assigned to specific administrators or teams based on their expertise, availability, or other factors. This helps ensure that each incident gets the attention it needs and can expedite the resolution process. The assignment process can be manual or automated, based on predefined rules or algorithms.
2. Priority Level Setting: Not all incidents are equally urgent or impactful. Setting priority levels for incidents helps to manage resources effectively and ensure that critical incidents are addressed promptly. The priority level can be based on factors such as the severity of the incident, its impact on the system or business processes, and the risk of it escalating if not addressed immediately.
3. Progress Tracking: As administrators work on resolving incidents, they can update the incident record with notes on the steps taken, findings, and current status. This helps to track the progress of resolution efforts, facilitates collaboration and communication among teams, and provides a record for future reference.
4. Time Tracking: Tracking the time spent on each incident is crucial for performance metrics, resource planning, and cost management. This can involve recording the time when an incident was reported, when it was assigned, when work began on it, and when it was resolved.
5. Resolution Recording: Once an incident is resolved, the resolution details are recorded in the incident log. This

typically includes a description of the resolution, the steps taken to achieve it, any changes made to the system, and possibly follow-up actions or recommendations to prevent the incident from recurring. This resolution record is invaluable for knowledge management and for improving system reliability and incident response processes.

6. Incident Reporting: Lastly, z/OSMF provides reporting features that can generate various reports based on the incident tracking data. These reports can be used for reviewing performance, identifying trends or issues, supporting decision-making, and communicating with stakeholders.

In conclusion, Incident Tracking plays a critical role in effective system management, helping to ensure prompt and effective response to incidents, and providing valuable data for improving system performance and reliability.

4. Incident Resolution

INCIDENT RESOLUTION is the final stage of incident management where the identified problem gets solved, and the system returns to normal operation. The resolution process in z/OSMF Incident Log Management can involve the following aspects:

1. Problem Solving Tools: z/OSMF provides a range of built-in tools that administrators can use to solve problems. Depending on the nature of the incident, these tools could include things like debuggers, performance analyzers, system tuners, or software update managers. The use of these tools would be based on the detailed analysis of the incident and the system's current state.
2. Solution Suggestions: Based on the incident details and possibly the history of similar incidents, z/OSMF can offer suggestions for solutions. This feature leverages IBM's deep experience with system management and its database of incident knowledge to propose potential ways to resolve the incident.
3. Automated Resolution: In some cases, z/OSMF may be able to resolve incidents automatically. This would typically involve known issues where a standard solution has been proven to work. For example, if a service crashes due to a resource shortage, z/OSMF might be able to automatically allocate more resources and restart the service.
4. Resource and Documentation Direction: When a complex issue arises, or a less common incident occurs, z/OSMF can point administrators to the relevant resources or IBM documentation. This can help administrators better understand the problem and find the appropriate solutions.
5. Incident Closure: After the problem is resolved, the incident

gets closed in the system. Details about the resolution, including steps taken, resources used, and the time taken to solve the issue are recorded. This information can be beneficial for future incident management and for organizational learning.

6. Preventive Measures: As part of the resolution process, z/OSMF also helps identify preventive measures to avoid the recurrence of the same issues in the future. This could involve changes to system configurations, software updates, or improvements in operational procedures.

In summary, z/OSMF's incident resolution capabilities provide a comprehensive and structured approach to restoring system functionality, learning from incidents, and improving system reliability and resilience.

5. Reporting

REPORTING IS A CRITICAL component of the incident log management process within z/OSMF. This feature allows for the extraction, compilation, and presentation of data from the incident logs into understandable and actionable formats. Let's break down the various aspects of the reporting feature:

1. Incident Reports: These reports compile details about specific incidents that have occurred over a given time period. These details can include the type of incident, the systems or services affected, the time it took to resolve the incident, the cause of the incident, and the solution implemented.
2. Trend Analysis: Reports can be generated to identify trends in the occurrence of incidents. This analysis can highlight recurring incidents, peak times for incidents, and correlations between different incidents. This insight can be useful for identifying underlying issues or for forecasting future incidents.
3. System Health Reports: These reports provide a broader view of the system's health, using data from the incident logs as well as other system data. These reports might include metrics like system uptime, availability of resources, performance metrics, and the frequency and impact of incidents.
4. Stakeholder Communication: Reports can be used to communicate the state of the system to various stakeholders. For example, executive reports can provide a high-level view of system health and stability, technical reports can provide in-depth details for IT staff, and regulatory reports can provide compliance information for auditors.
5. Planning and Decision Making: Incident reports and trend

analysis can provide valuable information for planning and decision making. This could involve decisions about system updates, hardware upgrades, capacity planning, or changes to system management processes.

6. Customizable Reports: z/OSMF allows for the creation of customizable reports. This means that administrators can define what data to include, how to format the report, and what period to cover. This flexibility allows administrators to generate reports that are tailored to their specific needs and those of their organization.

In summary, reporting in z/OSMF's Incident Log Management helps administrators understand past incidents, communicate effectively, make data-driven decisions, and plan for the future.

6.2 Workflow Management

THE WORKFLOW MANAGEMENT service is a significant component of z/OS Management Facility (z/OSMF) that helps automate, streamline, and simplify complex tasks in a mainframe environment. Here are the key aspects:

1. Workflow Creation: The initial step in workflow management is to create a workflow. A workflow is a defined series of steps meant to accomplish a specific task or set of tasks. These can be simple processes or complex ones that involve various dependencies and conditions. Workflows can be created by administrators and saved as templates for future use.
2. Workflow Execution: After a workflow is created, it can be executed, either manually by a user or automatically based on a specific trigger or schedule. During execution, z/OSMF manages the entire process, ensuring that each step is completed in the correct order and that any conditions or dependencies are met.
3. Step Management: Each workflow is composed of multiple steps, which are individual tasks within the workflow. Steps can be executed sequentially, in parallel, or conditionally based on the outcomes of other steps. Some steps may require manual intervention, while others can be fully automated.
4. Variable Substitution: Workflows in z/OSMF can utilize variables, which can be replaced with specific values at runtime. This allows the same workflow to be used in different situations or contexts, with the variables providing the necessary customization.
5. Workflow Monitoring: Once a workflow is executed, z/OSMF provides tools for monitoring its progress. This can

include viewing the status of each step, checking the overall progress of the workflow, and receiving alerts or notifications about any issues or errors that occur.

6. Workflow Control: Beyond monitoring, z/OSMF also provides controls for managing running workflows. This includes the ability to pause, resume, or stop a workflow, as well as the ability to manually intervene in a step if necessary.
7. Reporting and Auditing: z/OSMF can generate reports about workflow execution, including details about each step, any issues or errors that occurred, and the overall completion status. This data can be used for auditing purposes, for troubleshooting, or for improving future workflows.

In essence, the Workflow Management service in z/OSMF provides a powerful and flexible tool for automating and managing tasks in a mainframe environment, helping to improve efficiency, reduce errors, and provide better visibility and control over processes.

1. Workflow Creation

WORKFLOW CREATION IN z/OSMF involves planning and defining the series of tasks required to complete a specific business process or operation within the mainframe environment. This is a crucial aspect of the Workflow Management system as it provides a structured approach to automate and streamline complex tasks. Here's how it works:

1. Define the Objective: Before a workflow can be created, the specific objective or task it is meant to accomplish must be clearly defined. This could be anything from deploying a new application, performing system maintenance, or automating a regular report.
2. Identify Tasks and Dependencies: After defining the objective, the next step is to break it down into individual tasks. Each task in a workflow represents a single unit of work. In more complex workflows, tasks may have dependencies, which means the execution of one task depends on the completion of another.
3. Create Workflow Steps: Using the identified tasks and dependencies, you then construct a sequence of steps that make up the workflow. Each step is configured with the necessary information required for its execution, such as commands to be run, scripts to be executed, or input parameters required.
4. Set Conditions: In some cases, a step may only need to be executed under certain conditions. Conditional execution of steps can be configured in the workflow. For instance, a step to rollback changes can be set to execute only if a previous step fails.
5. Specify Variables: Variables can be used in workflows to

represent data that may change each time the workflow is executed. For instance, a variable might represent the name of a file to be processed or the date a task should run.

6. Save Workflow Template: Once the workflow is fully defined, it can be saved as a template. These templates can be used to create new workflows with the same structure, which can save time and ensure consistency when performing similar tasks in the future.

With this process, z/OSMF allows administrators to model complex processes in a way that can be reliably repeated, reducing the possibility for human error and improving overall efficiency in mainframe operations.

2. Workflow Execution

WORKFLOW EXECUTION in z/OSMF is the process where the previously defined and saved workflow is run to achieve its intended task. z/OSMF handles the complexity of managing the workflow, ensuring tasks are performed in the right sequence and conditions are met. Here's how the process works:

1. Initiation: Workflow execution can be initiated either manually by an administrator or automatically. Automatic initiation could be based on specific triggers (such as a particular event happening in the system) or on a pre-defined schedule (like a certain time of day or day of the week).
2. Step Execution: Once the workflow has been initiated, z/OSMF starts executing the steps in the workflow in the order they have been defined. For each step, it initiates the necessary tasks, which could include running scripts, executing commands, or performing other operations.
3. Dependency Handling: If there are dependencies between steps, z/OSMF ensures these are properly handled. It will only execute a step if all its dependencies have been successfully completed. This ensures the integrity of the workflow and helps prevent errors.
4. Condition Checking: If there are conditions defined for a step, z/OSMF checks these before executing the step. The step is only executed if the conditions are met. This allows for complex workflows that can adapt to different situations or system states.
5. Error Handling: In case of an error or failure in any step, z/OSMF handles it according to the predefined error handling procedures in the workflow. This could include skipping the step, stopping the whole workflow, or rolling back previous

steps.

6. Logging and Monitoring: Throughout the execution of the workflow, z/OSMF logs information about the progress of each step. This allows administrators to monitor the workflow execution and helps in troubleshooting in case of errors. The logs also provide a record of what actions were performed, which can be important for auditing purposes.
7. Completion: Once all steps have been executed (assuming no errors that stop the workflow), the workflow execution is completed. z/OSMF will then update the status of the workflow and notify the relevant administrators, if necessary.

This robust execution process makes z/OSMF a powerful tool for automating and managing complex tasks in a mainframe environment.

3. Step Management

STEP MANAGEMENT IN the context of workflow management with z/OSMF involves creating, configuring, and controlling the individual tasks that make up a workflow. Each step in the workflow is a single task that needs to be accomplished as part of the overall process. Let's look at some key elements of step management:

1. Step Creation: When creating a workflow, the administrator defines each step that needs to be carried out to complete the process. Each step includes details such as the task to be performed, the input required, the expected output, and any error handling procedures.
2. Sequential Execution: Steps can be set to execute in a specific sequence, which is the most common mode of execution. The workflow moves from one step to the next in the order defined during the creation process.
3. Parallel Execution: In some workflows, certain steps can be performed simultaneously. These are typically steps that are independent of each other and do not have any dependencies. z/OSMF allows for the configuration of such parallel steps, improving efficiency and reducing the overall time taken to complete the workflow.
4. Conditional Execution: z/OSMF allows for steps to be executed based on specific conditions. This can be based on the outcome of a previous step or some other predefined conditions. For example, if a step in a workflow is to check the available storage, the next step could be conditionally set to either clean up storage (if space is low) or proceed to the next task (if sufficient space exists).
5. Manual vs. Automated Steps: While many steps in a workflow can be automated, some may require manual

intervention. This could be necessary for tasks that require judgment or decision-making. z/OSMF allows for the configuration of both manual and automated steps in a workflow, providing flexibility in how tasks are managed.

6. Step Monitoring and Control: Administrators can monitor the progress of individual steps in a workflow using the z/OSMF interface. If necessary, administrators can also intervene to pause, stop, or restart steps.

By providing robust step management capabilities, z/OSMF allows administrators to design and manage complex workflows that can automate many tasks in a z/OS environment.

4. Variable Substitution

VARIABLE SUBSTITUTION plays a critical role in enhancing the flexibility and reusability of workflows in z/OSMF. The idea is to define parts of a workflow in a generic way and then substitute those parts with specific values at runtime. Here are the key points:

1. Variable Definition: Variables are defined during the workflow creation process. They are typically represented as placeholders within the workflow. The placeholder values are then replaced by actual values at runtime.
2. Runtime Substitution: When a workflow is started, the user is typically prompted to provide values for the defined variables. These values are then used to replace the placeholders throughout the workflow. This process is called variable substitution.
3. Customization: Variable substitution allows the same workflow to be used in different contexts or scenarios. For instance, a workflow designed to install software can have a variable representing the software package's location. By substitifying the variable with different values, the same workflow can be used to install different software packages.
4. Dynamic Workflow Modification: Variables can also be used to dynamically modify the behavior of a workflow based on specific conditions. For example, a workflow could include a decision-making step that sets the value of a variable, which then determines which subsequent steps are executed.
5. Reduced Errors: By reducing the need to manually input information each time a workflow is run, variable substitution can also reduce the possibility of errors that could occur due to manual input.

In conclusion, Variable Substitution is a powerful feature in z/OSMF that provides the ability to create flexible, customizable, and reusable workflows that can cater to various scenarios and tasks in the z/OS environment.

5. Workflow Monitoring

WORKFLOW MONITORING is an essential part of the z/OS Management Facility (z/OSMF). It allows administrators to supervise the status and progress of workflows in real-time. Here's a more detailed description:

1. Step Status: In z/OSMF, each workflow consists of multiple steps. During the workflow execution, it's possible to monitor the status of each step. The status can vary - some steps might be completed, some could be in progress, while others are yet to start. This granular visibility allows users to pinpoint exactly where a workflow is at any given time.
2. Progress Overview: Apart from tracking individual steps, z/OSMF also provides an overall progress overview of the workflow. This summary-style information can be useful to quickly ascertain how far along a workflow is and how much more needs to be done.
3. Error Alerts and Notifications: If there are any issues or errors during the execution of a workflow, z/OSMF can provide alerts or notifications. These can be in the form of on-screen messages, emails, or other types of notifications depending on the system setup. These alerts can provide immediate visibility into problems, allowing for rapid response and issue resolution.
4. Log Analysis: z/OSMF workflow monitoring also includes the ability to review and analyze logs generated during workflow execution. These logs can provide valuable information for troubleshooting and optimization.
5. Performance Metrics: Some advanced workflow monitoring setups might also track performance metrics, such as the execution time for each step or the overall workflow, resource

utilization, etc. These metrics can help identify bottlenecks and improve workflow efficiency.

In essence, Workflow Monitoring in z/OSMF is a powerful tool that provides real-time visibility into workflow execution, enabling administrators to track progress, troubleshoot issues, and optimize workflow efficiency.

6. Workflow Control

WORKFLOW CONTROL IN z/OS Management Facility (z/OSMF) provides users with several capabilities to manage the execution of workflows beyond simply monitoring their progress. These control features include:

1. Pause: A running workflow can be paused at any time. This halts the execution of the workflow at its current step, allowing administrators to suspend the process temporarily. This could be useful in a variety of scenarios, such as during system maintenance windows, to conserve system resources, or if there is a need to check or alter something in the system before allowing the workflow to proceed.
2. Resume: After a workflow has been paused, it can be resumed at the same point where it was stopped. This allows the process to continue from exactly where it left off, ensuring that no steps are skipped or repeated.
3. Stop: If a workflow needs to be halted permanently before it completes, the 'Stop' function can be used. Stopping a workflow generally means it cannot be resumed from the same point, and to restart the workflow, it would typically need to be initiated from the beginning.
4. Manual Intervention: Some workflows may require manual steps, or there might be a need for an administrator to intervene in an automated step under certain conditions. z/OSMF provides the ability for users to interact with running workflows, to perform manual steps when necessary, or to adjust the behavior of the workflow based on the current state of the system.
5. Step Override: In certain situations, it may be necessary to override the default behavior of a workflow step. This could

involve skipping a step, forcing a step to be executed even if its conditions aren't met, or changing the execution order of the steps.

6. Workflow Restart: In cases where a workflow is stopped (either intentionally or due to an error), z/OSMF allows users to restart the workflow. Depending on the workflow's design and the system's configuration, it may be possible to restart the workflow from the beginning or from a specific step.

These control features provide a high degree of flexibility and control over workflow execution in z/OSMF, allowing administrators to efficiently manage workflows to meet their specific needs or the unique requirements of their system environment.

7. Reporting and Auditing

REPORTING AND AUDITING in z/OSMF plays a crucial role in evaluating workflow execution and maintaining a high level of system accountability and transparency. Here's a detailed explanation of these functionalities:

1. Reporting: Reporting is an essential tool for providing insights into the execution of workflows. Post-execution, z/OSMF can generate comprehensive reports that include detailed information about each executed step, including start and end times, any input or output data, and the success or failure status of each step. This can be particularly useful for reviewing the efficiency of the workflow, identifying bottlenecks or issues, and documenting the process for future reference. In addition, these reports can provide insights into the utilization of system resources, allowing for optimization of future workflows.
2. Error Reporting: In addition to general reporting, z/OSMF places a special emphasis on error reporting. If a workflow fails at any step or encounters an unexpected condition, detailed error messages are logged and included in the report. This can provide invaluable information for troubleshooting purposes, helping to identify exactly what went wrong and where, which can assist in correcting the issue for future runs.
3. Auditing: Beyond just providing insight, these reports can also serve as a crucial part of an auditing process. Each step of the workflow execution is logged, creating a detailed trail of actions and changes. This can help ensure compliance with internal policies or external regulations, as well as maintain accountability. An auditor, for instance, can examine these logs to verify that all actions were carried out correctly and by

authorized personnel.

4. Improvement: Lastly, the data from reporting and auditing can be used to improve future workflows. By identifying steps that consistently fail or take longer than expected, administrators can redesign workflows to avoid these issues in the future, improving efficiency and reliability.

In summary, reporting and auditing capabilities in z/OSMF not only provide valuable insights into the execution of workflows but also enable continuous system improvement and ensure compliance with regulatory standards.

6.3 Configuration Assistant

THE CONFIGURATION ASSISTANT is a feature of z/OS Management Facility (z/OSMF) that simplifies the management of system configuration data. It's an essential part of z/OSMF, providing an interface for managing a wide range of configuration tasks. Here's a more detailed breakdown of its functionalities:

1. Configuration Data Management: The Configuration Assistant allows administrators to view, modify, and manage the configuration data for various system components. This includes things like network settings, system parameters, device settings, and more. It provides an intuitive graphical interface for managing this data, making it easier to understand and modify system configurations.
2. Configuration Profiles: The Configuration Assistant allows the creation and management of configuration profiles. These are sets of configuration data that can be applied to a system or a component. By using profiles, administrators can quickly and easily switch between different configurations, or apply a known good configuration to troubleshoot issues.
3. Version Control: The Configuration Assistant can track different versions of configuration data. This allows administrators to easily roll back changes if a problem occurs. It also provides a history of configuration changes, which can be useful for auditing purposes or for troubleshooting configuration issues.
4. Validation and Verification: The Configuration Assistant can validate configuration changes to ensure they're consistent and correct. This can help prevent errors before they cause problems. Once changes are made, the Configuration Assistant can also verify that the new settings are in effect and

working correctly.

5. Integration with Other z/OSMF Services: The Configuration Assistant works together with other z/OSMF services. For example, it can utilize workflows to automate the process of making configuration changes, or it can use the incident log management service to log any issues that occur during the configuration process.

In summary, the Configuration Assistant in z/OSMF is a comprehensive tool for managing system configurations, providing features for managing configuration data, handling configuration profiles, controlling versions, and validating and verifying configuration changes.

1. Configuration Data Management

CONFIGURATION DATA Management is the essential function of the Configuration Assistant. It gives you an organized view of system components and their settings, and provides the tools necessary to manage these configurations. Here's more detail on its functionalities:

1. Viewing Configuration Data: The Configuration Assistant provides a clear and structured view of configuration data for different system components. This could be anything from system parameters and network settings, to device configurations. This simplifies the task of understanding the current system configurations, which can otherwise be complex and difficult to comprehend.
2. Modifying Configuration Data: Not only can you view the configuration data, but you can also modify it directly from the Configuration Assistant. The user-friendly interface allows administrators to make changes to the settings easily, eliminating the need to use complicated commands or navigate through numerous system files.
3. Managing Configuration Data: On top of viewing and modifying data, the Configuration Assistant also provides functions for managing configuration data. This could involve creating or deleting configurations, copying configurations between different systems or components, or setting up schedules for applying certain configurations.
4. Intuitive Graphical Interface: One of the key benefits of the Configuration Assistant is its graphical interface. It provides a visual representation of the configuration data, making it easier to understand. This interface can include tables, charts, or diagrams, and it allows administrators to interact with the configuration data in a more intuitive way.

5. In-Depth Information: The Configuration Assistant provides in-depth information about each configuration setting. When viewing or modifying a configuration, you can access detailed information about what each setting does, what values it can have, and how it affects the system. This can be invaluable for administrators, especially when dealing with unfamiliar settings or troubleshooting issues.

Through these features, the Configuration Assistant allows administrators to effectively manage the complex configuration data of their z/OS systems. It simplifies the task of understanding, modifying, and managing configurations, and provides the necessary tools and information to do so effectively.

2. Configuration Profiles

CONFIGURATION PROFILES are a key feature of the Configuration Assistant in z/OSMF. These profiles are essentially "snapshots" of configuration data that can be applied to a system or its components. They make it easy to manage different configurations and provide a more flexible way to administer system settings. Let's break down how they function:

1. Creation of Configuration Profiles: With the Configuration Assistant, administrators can create configuration profiles. This involves selecting specific configuration data and saving it as a profile. This could be a set of settings that are known to work well, or a configuration for a specific use-case or scenario.
2. Management of Configuration Profiles: Once created, these configuration profiles can be managed within the Configuration Assistant. This management includes renaming, deleting, copying, or modifying existing profiles. This makes it easy to organize and manage different configurations for different use-cases, environments, or system components.
3. Application of Configuration Profiles: Configuration profiles are not just for storage – they can be actively applied to a system or its components. This means that the system's configuration can be quickly and easily changed by simply selecting a different profile. This can be particularly useful in situations where the configuration needs to be changed frequently or rapidly, such as in testing or development environments.
4. Troubleshooting and Recovery: Configuration profiles can also serve as a recovery mechanism. If something goes wrong

with a system's configuration, administrators can quickly revert to a known good configuration by applying an appropriate profile. This can significantly reduce downtime in the event of a configuration error.

5. Sharing and Distribution: In larger environments with multiple systems or components, configuration profiles can be shared or distributed across these systems. This ensures consistency in configuration across an environment and reduces the time and effort needed to manually configure each system or component.

By providing a flexible and efficient way to manage configurations, Configuration Profiles can greatly simplify the task of system administration in complex z/OS environments.

3. Version Control

THE VERSION CONTROL capabilities of the Configuration Assistant in z/OSMF are crucial for maintaining system stability and for managing changes over time. They provide several important benefits for system administrators:

1. Change Tracking: Each time configuration data is altered and saved, the Configuration Assistant creates a new version of that data. This means that every change made to a configuration is tracked and documented, providing a clear record of who made what changes and when. This is critical for auditing purposes, for maintaining accountability, and for understanding the history of the system's configuration.
2. Rollback Capability: With version control, if a change to the system's configuration causes a problem or an error, administrators have the ability to "roll back" to a previous version. This means they can quickly and easily revert the system back to a state before the problematic change was introduced. This feature can dramatically reduce downtime caused by configuration errors and helps maintain system stability.
3. Comparison of Versions: The version control in Configuration Assistant also allows administrators to compare different versions of a configuration. This can be useful for identifying what changes were made between versions, which can help in troubleshooting issues, understanding the impact of specific changes, or planning future changes.
4. Preserving Stable Configurations: By saving stable, tested versions of configurations, administrators can ensure that they always have a safe set of configuration data to return to if

a new configuration causes problems. This also allows administrators to experiment with different configurations with less risk, as they can always return to a known-good state if necessary.

Overall, the version control capabilities of the Configuration Assistant provide a powerful tool for managing, tracking, and controlling changes to system configurations. It helps prevent problems caused by configuration changes and aids in maintaining the overall stability and reliability of the system.

4. Validation and Verification

THE VALIDATION AND Verification capabilities in Configuration Assistant of z/OSMF are critical features that help maintain system stability and functionality. These features are essentially about checking and confirming the correctness and effectiveness of configuration changes. Here's a deeper look at both aspects:

1. Validation: This process happens before a configuration change is applied to the system. It involves checking the new configuration data for any inconsistencies, errors, or violations of rules and standards. Validation can catch things like:
    - Typographical errors or format mistakes, such as entering an IP address in the wrong format.
    - Values that are out of the allowed range, like setting a memory allocation size bigger than the available memory.
    - Incompatible settings, such as enabling two features that can't be used together.
    - Violations of best practices or organizational policies, such as using weak security settings.

If any such issues are detected, the Configuration Assistant can alert the administrator and prevent the problematic changes from being applied, averting potential problems.

1. Verification: This process occurs after a configuration change has been made. It involves checking that the new settings have been correctly applied and are functioning as expected. For example, if a network setting was changed, the Configuration Assistant might run a connectivity test to

verify that the network is still functioning correctly. Verification helps ensure that changes have the intended effect and that no unexpected side effects have occurred.

The combination of validation and verification provides a robust system for managing configuration changes. By catching errors before they're applied and confirming the success of changes after they're made, these features help to maintain the system's stability, performance, and security.

5. Integration with Other z/OSMF Services

THE CONFIGURATION ASSISTANT in z/OSMF does not operate in isolation. It's designed to work in concert with other services within the z/OSMF ecosystem to provide a comprehensive, integrated system management experience. Let's explore how this works with a few key examples:

1. Integration with Workflow Management: Workflow Management in z/OSMF allows administrators to define a series of steps to accomplish a specific task. These workflows can be used to automate many aspects of system management, including configuration changes. For instance, you could create a workflow to automatically apply a specific configuration profile to a set of systems, validate the changes, and then perform some tests to verify the new configuration.

   This integration can help streamline the process of making configuration changes, ensure that changes are made consistently across multiple systems, and reduce the risk of human error.

2. Integration with Incident Log Management: The Configuration Assistant can utilize the Incident Log Management service to record any issues or anomalies that occur during the configuration process. For example, if a configuration change fails or causes an error, this can be automatically logged as an incident. Administrators can then use the incident log to investigate the problem, identify its cause, and take corrective action.

In addition to logging incidents, the Configuration Assistant can also use the Incident Log Management service to access historical incident data. This can provide valuable context when making configuration changes. For instance, if a certain type of configuration change has caused issues in the past, this information could inform the validation and verification processes, helping to prevent similar issues from occurring in the future.

3. Integration with Other Services: Depending on the specific needs and setup of your z/OS environment, the Configuration Assistant can potentially interact with other z/OSMF services as well. For example, it might use the Resource Monitoring service to check system resource usage before making configuration changes, or it could work with the Software Management service to manage the configuration of installed software packages.

Through these integrations, the Configuration Assistant is able to leverage the capabilities of other z/OSMF services, enhancing its own functionality and contributing to a more cohesive and effective system management solution.

Chapter 7: Advanced z/OSMF Features

In addition to the core features and services we've already discussed, z/OSMF also offers several advanced features that can provide additional capabilities and extend the platform's functionality.

7.1 Plug-ins and Extensions: z/OSMF supports plug-ins and extensions that can add new features or services to the platform. These can be developed by IBM, by third-party vendors, or even by users themselves. Plug-ins and extensions can greatly increase the versatility of z/OSMF, allowing it to support a wider range of system management tasks and cater to specific needs or requirements.

7.2 Capacity Provisioning: This feature provides tools and services for managing the capacity of your z/OS systems. This includes features for monitoring system resource usage, predicting future capacity needs, and dynamically allocating resources to meet those needs. With capacity provisioning, you can ensure that your z/OS systems are making optimal use of their resources and are able to handle changes in workload or demand.

7.3 REST APIs in z/OSMF: z/OSMF provides REST APIs that allow other software to interact with its services. This can be used to automate system management tasks, to integrate z/OSMF with other software or systems, or to develop custom applications that utilize z/OSMF's services. With the REST APIs, you can leverage the power of z/OSMF in a wide range of contexts and applications.

These advanced features enable z/OSMF to cater to a wide range of system management needs and scenarios, making it a versatile and powerful tool for managing z/OS environments.

7.1 Plug-ins and Extensions

PLUG-INS AND EXTENSIONS in z/OS Management Facility (z/OSMF) provide added functionalities to the base system. These allow the system to perform specialized tasks and increase the overall utility of z/OSMF. Here's a deeper look into these features:

1. Plug-in Installation: Installing a plug-in or extension is the first step to extending the functionality of z/OSMF. These plug-ins can be provided by IBM, third-party vendors, or they can be custom-developed depending on the specific needs of your organization. Once installed, these plug-ins become part of the z/OSMF environment and can be managed just like any other part of the system.
2. Plug-in Functionality: Plug-ins and extensions can add a wide variety of functionalities to z/OSMF. For example, a plug-in could provide tools for managing specific types of hardware, or it could add new interfaces or APIs for interacting with external systems. The possibilities are virtually limitless, as the plug-in functionality is only constrained by what can be programmed.
3. Integration with z/OSMF Services: After a plug-in is installed, it's not isolated - it can interact with and utilize the services provided by z/OSMF. For instance, a plug-in might use z/OSMF's workflow management services to automate its tasks, or it might use the incident log management services to record and analyze any issues it encounters.
4. Plug-in Management: Just like the core z/OSMF services, plug-ins can be managed from within the z/OSMF interface. This includes configuring the plug-in, monitoring its operation, troubleshooting any issues, and updating or uninstalling the plug-in as needed.

5. Extending z/OSMF Capabilities: Ultimately, the main purpose of plug-ins and extensions is to extend the capabilities of z/OSMF. By adding new features and services, plug-ins can tailor z/OSMF to better suit the specific needs and requirements of your organization, making the system a more effective and efficient tool for managing your z/OS environment.

1. Plug-in Installation

THE PLUG-INS FOR Z/OSMF are pieces of software that, once installed, provide additional functionality or capabilities to the main z/OSMF system. These plugins can come from a variety of sources. Some are developed by IBM to offer additional services, others may come from third-party vendors, and in some cases, organizations might develop their own custom plugins to meet specific needs not covered by the existing offerings.

When a new plug-in is to be installed, it's crucial to follow the provided installation instructions precisely, as each plug-in may have unique installation procedures. The instructions typically come in the form of documentation supplied by the plug-in's developer and usually involve copying the necessary files to the correct locations, setting up any required configuration parameters, and possibly running installation scripts.

Once a plug-in is installed, it's integrated into the z/OSMF environment. This means it can be accessed through the z/OSMF interface, and its functions can be used as if they were a part of the core z/OSMF system. This seamless integration simplifies usage and provides a consistent user experience.

Moreover, installed plug-ins can be managed using the same system management tools that are used for the rest of z/OSMF. This includes things like monitoring the plugin's performance, configuring its settings, or updating it to a newer version. This makes it easier for system administrators to maintain the entire system, including all of its plugins, ensuring that everything operates smoothly and efficiently.

In conclusion, plug-in installation is a key aspect of customizing and extending the functionality of z/OSMF. It allows organizations to tailor the system to their specific needs, improving their ability to manage their mainframe resources effectively.

2. Plug-in Functionality

THE POWER OF PLUGINS lies in their ability to extend the capabilities of z/OSMF in countless ways. The specific functionality that a plug-in adds depends on its purpose and design. Here are some examples of the types of features and capabilities that plugins might offer:

- Hardware Management: Some plugins are designed to manage specific types of hardware that are part of the mainframe environment. This might include tools for configuring the hardware, monitoring its performance, managing firmware updates, or diagnosing hardware-related issues.
- Interfaces and APIs: Plugins can also add new interfaces or APIs to z/OSMF. This could include web-based interfaces that allow users to interact with z/OSMF from a browser, command-line interfaces for scripting or automation purposes, or APIs that allow external systems or applications to interact with z/OSMF programmatically.
- Application Management: Some plugins focus on managing specific applications or services that run on the mainframe. This could involve application-specific monitoring tools, configuration management features, or tools for deploying and updating the application.
- Data Management: Plugins might provide tools for managing the data stored on the mainframe, including databases, filesystems, or data sets. This could include tools for data backup and recovery, data replication, data compression, or data migration.
- Security Features: Some plugins add additional security features to z/OSMF. This might include tools for managing

encryption keys, managing user access controls, auditing security events, or scanning for security vulnerabilities.

In essence, the functionality added by a plugin depends on what the plugin is designed to do. The only real limitation is that the plugin must be able to interact with z/OSMF and the mainframe environment, and it must adhere to the conventions and standards required for z/OSMF plugins. Other than that, a plugin can provide almost any functionality that can be achieved through programming.

3. Integration with z/OSMF Services

PLUG-INS ARE INTEGRATED into the z/OSMF environment, which means they have the ability to interact with and leverage the services provided by z/OSMF. This integration can lead to more powerful and flexible tools for managing your mainframe system. Here's a deeper look into how plug-ins can utilize z/OSMF services:

- Workflow Management Services: z/OSMF's workflow management services are a powerful tool for automating tasks. If a plug-in has tasks that need to be performed regularly or under specific conditions, it could use these workflow management services to automate these tasks. This could involve creating a workflow that performs the task, and then setting a trigger or schedule that determines when the workflow is executed. By integrating with the workflow management services, plug-ins can automate their operations, reducing the need for manual intervention and increasing efficiency.
- Incident Log Management Services: The incident log management services provided by z/OSMF offer a way for plug-ins to log and analyze incidents. When an issue occurs within a plug-in, it can log this incident using these services. This log entry can include details about the incident, such as what happened, when it happened, what part of the system was affected, and any error messages that were generated. This information can then be used to analyze the incident, identify its cause, and resolve it. By integrating with these services, plug-ins can effectively handle issues and reduce downtime.
- Configuration Assistant: The Configuration Assistant is a tool provided by z/OSMF for managing system

configuration data. If a plug-in needs to modify system configurations or manage its own configuration data, it could integrate with the Configuration Assistant to do so. This could involve reading or modifying configuration profiles, managing versions of configuration data, or validating and verifying configuration changes. This integration can make it easier for plug-ins to manage configurations and reduce the risk of configuration errors.

In summary, by integrating with z/OSMF services, plug-ins can utilize the powerful tools provided by z/OSMF to improve their functionality, automate their operations, manage incidents, and handle configurations. This makes plug-ins a versatile tool for enhancing the capabilities of your z/OSMF system.

4. Plug-in Management

PLUG-INS, ONCE INSTALLED into the z/OSMF environment, are not just standalone entities. They become an integrated part of the z/OSMF system and, as such, they can be managed just as one would manage the core components of the system. Here are some key aspects of plug-in management:

- Configuration: Each plug-in that's installed into the z/OSMF environment comes with its own set of configurations. These configurations can be managed within the z/OSMF interface. For instance, this could involve setting up initial parameters, adjusting settings as per requirements, or making changes in response to evolving needs or circumstances.
- Monitoring: In addition to configuration, the operation of plug-ins can also be monitored within z/OSMF. This can include observing the status of the plug-in, examining the tasks it's performing, or checking its resource usage. This monitoring can help ensure the plug-in is operating correctly and efficiently.
- Troubleshooting: If a plug-in encounters an issue, the z/OSMF interface can provide tools for troubleshooting. This can involve checking the incident logs for any relevant entries, running diagnostic tools, or adjusting configurations to resolve the issue. In many cases, the ability to troubleshoot issues directly within z/OSMF can lead to quicker resolution times.
- Updating or Uninstalling: Plug-ins, just like any software, may need to be updated from time to time. This could be to add new features, improve performance, or fix bugs. These updates can often be managed within the z/OSMF interface.

Similarly, if a plug-in is no longer needed or if it's causing issues, it can be uninstalled through the z/OSMF interface.

In conclusion, plug-in management in z/OSMF is a comprehensive process, encompassing everything from initial configuration to monitoring, troubleshooting, and updating or uninstalling. This level of integration allows for a seamless experience in extending the functionality and efficiency of the z/OSMF environment.

5. Extending z/OSMF Capabilities

PLUG-INS AND EXTENSIONS provide a crucial means of tailoring the z/OSMF environment to suit the specific needs and workflows of an organization. Here's how they contribute to extending z/OSMF capabilities:

- Custom Functionality: Each organization has unique requirements, and often these may not be fully addressed by the standard features offered by z/OSMF. Plug-ins and extensions can add specific functionality or features that address these unique needs, thereby enhancing the utility of z/OSMF for that organization.
- Improved Efficiency: With custom plug-ins, repetitive or complex tasks can be automated, thus saving valuable time and reducing the risk of errors. This leads to improved operational efficiency and can free up your system administrators to focus on more strategic, high-value tasks.
- Enhanced Integration: If your organization uses other software tools or systems in addition to z/OS, plug-ins can be used to enhance integration between these systems and z/OSMF. This allows for smoother data flow, easier management of tasks, and improved overall system operation.
- Tailored User Experience: Plug-ins and extensions can also tailor the user experience to better suit your organization's preferences or workflows. This can include changes to the interface, addition of new controls, or modifications to how data is displayed.
- Addressing Future Needs: As your organization evolves, so too will its requirements. The ability to install new plug-ins or update existing ones means that z/OSMF can adapt to meet these changing needs, ensuring it remains a powerful

tool for system management.

In summary, by adding new functionalities and services, plug-ins and extensions significantly enhance z/OSMF's capabilities. They allow for a more customized, efficient, and future-ready management of your z/OS environment.

7.2 Capacity Provisioning

CAPACITY PROVISIONING in z/OSMF refers to the dynamic and automated allocation and de-allocation of system resources such as processing power, memory, storage, and network bandwidth. This is crucial for effective system management and maintaining optimal performance levels. Here's a deeper dive into this:

1. Demand-Driven Provisioning: z/OSMF can automatically adjust system capacity based on current demand and predefined policies. This can ensure that critical applications always have the resources they need to function effectively, while non-critical tasks are relegated to times when system load is lower.
2. Proactive Resource Allocation: Using historical data and predictive analytics, z/OSMF can anticipate future resource needs and allocate capacity proactively. This can reduce the risk of system overloads and ensure smooth and uninterrupted operation.
3. Resource Pooling and Virtualization: z/OSMF's capacity provisioning features can pool together system resources and allocate them dynamically to different applications or users. This can involve virtualizing physical resources, which can make the system more flexible and efficient.
4. Policy-Based Management: Administrators can define policies that dictate how system resources are allocated. These policies can be based on a variety of factors, including the importance of different tasks, usage patterns, performance targets, and more. z/OSMF can then enforce these policies automatically.
5. Performance Monitoring and Adjustments: z/OSMF continuously monitors system performance and makes

adjustments to capacity allocation as needed. This can involve shifting resources between different tasks, adding or removing resources from the pool, or adjusting the parameters of virtual resources.

6. Reporting and Analytics: Finally, z/OSMF provides detailed reports and analytics on capacity usage, performance metrics, and provisioning activities. This data can be used for capacity planning, performance optimization, and troubleshooting.

In conclusion, capacity provisioning in z/OSMF provides a dynamic and automated approach to resource management, helping organizations get the most out of their mainframe systems.

1. Demand-Driven Provisioning:

THE DEMAND-DRIVEN PROVISIONING is a key feature of z/OSMF that facilitates a more effective and efficient use of system resources. Here's a deeper look into how it works:

- Dynamic Resource Allocation: This feature allows z/OSMF to allocate system resources dynamically, based on the current demand. This can include things like processing power, memory, or I/O capacity. When demand for a particular resource increases, z/OSMF can allocate more of that resource to handle the increased load. Conversely, when demand decreases, those resources can be freed up for other tasks.
- Policy-Driven: The decision on how and when to adjust system capacity is based on predefined policies set by system administrators. These policies define things like the maximum and minimum resource levels for certain tasks, the priorities of different tasks, and the conditions under which resources should be reallocated.
- Ensuring Performance: The primary goal of demand-driven provisioning is to ensure that critical tasks have the resources they need to perform optimally. By dynamically adjusting resources, z/OSMF can ensure that these tasks don't suffer from resource shortages, which could lead to decreased performance or system instability.
- Efficient Use of Resources: Demand-driven provisioning also helps to ensure that system resources are used efficiently. By adjusting resource levels based on demand, z/OSMF can prevent resources from being wasted on low-priority tasks when they could be better used elsewhere. This can also help to reduce costs, as it ensures that you're getting the most out

of your system resources.

- Flexibility: With demand-driven provisioning, your z/OS system can better adapt to changes in workload or business needs. Whether you're dealing with a sudden surge in demand or a long-term shift in your resource needs, z/OSMF can adjust system capacity as needed to handle the change.

2. Proactive Resource Allocation:

PROACTIVE RESOURCE allocation in z/OSMF provides an advanced approach to system management, allowing administrators to stay ahead of resource demands rather than merely reacting to them. This is how it works:

- Predictive Analytics: This approach involves the use of predictive analytics, which utilizes historical system data and statistical algorithms to forecast future resource needs. This is done by analyzing patterns in the historical data and applying these patterns to predict future behavior.
- Historical Data: The historical data that z/OSMF uses can include details about previous system loads, the performance of different tasks and services, and the past allocation and usage of resources. By analyzing this data, z/OSMF can identify trends and patterns that indicate future resource needs.
- Proactive Allocation: Based on these predictions, z/OSMF can allocate resources proactively, ensuring they are available when needed. This means that if the system predicts an increase in demand for a particular resource, it can allocate more of that resource ahead of time, thus preventing any potential performance issues or bottlenecks.
- Smoother Operation: This proactive approach helps to ensure smoother and more consistent system operation. By anticipating and preparing for changes in resource demand, z/OSMF can prevent sudden drops in performance or system overloads, leading to a more stable and reliable operating environment.
- Continuous Learning: As z/OSMF collects and analyzes more data over time, its predictions become more accurate

and its resource allocation more effective. This continuous learning process allows z/OSMF to adapt to changes in system behavior or workload patterns, further enhancing its proactive resource allocation capabilities.

3. Resource Pooling and Virtualization:

RESOURCE POOLING AND virtualization are key components of z/OSMF's capacity provisioning capabilities. These features allow for more flexible and efficient use of system resources. Let's explore these concepts in more detail:

- Resource Pooling: In a computing context, resource pooling involves aggregating the system's resources and managing them collectively, rather than as individual units. For instance, instead of assigning specific processors to specific tasks, all processors might be pooled together and their capacity shared amongst all tasks. This pooled capacity can then be allocated and reallocated dynamically as demands change. Pooling can apply to various resources, such as processing power, memory, storage, and network bandwidth.
- Dynamic Allocation: Dynamic allocation is a key advantage of resource pooling. When resources are pooled, z/OSMF can allocate them on-the-fly to meet current demands. For instance, if one task suddenly needs more processing power, z/OSMF can temporarily allocate more processors from the pool to that task. Once the demand subsides, these resources can be returned to the pool for use by other tasks. This dynamic allocation can help improve system utilization and performance.
- Virtualization: Virtualization involves creating virtual, rather than physical, versions of system resources. This can increase the flexibility and efficiency of resource allocation. For example, a single physical server can be virtualized into multiple virtual servers, each running its own tasks. z/OSMF can manage these virtual resources just like physical ones, dynamically allocating them from the pool based on current

demand.

- Improved Flexibility and Efficiency: By pooling and virtualizing resources, z/OSMF can make the system more flexible and efficient. Tasks can be allocated exactly the resources they need, when they need them, improving system utilization and reducing waste. Moreover, virtualization can allow for more tasks to be run on fewer physical resources, reducing hardware costs and energy usage.

Through these features, z/OSMF's capacity provisioning can help to ensure that the z/OS system has the resources it needs to operate effectively, while also making the most efficient use of available resources.

4. Policy-Based Management:

POLICY-BASED MANAGEMENT is a key feature of z/OSMF's capacity provisioning capabilities. By allowing administrators to set policies that dictate how resources are allocated, the system can automate the resource management process while still adhering to the organization's specific needs and priorities. Let's delve deeper into this concept:

- Setting Policies: Administrators can define policies according to a variety of factors, including but not limited to, the relative importance or priority of different tasks or applications, historical usage patterns, performance targets, and availability requirements. For instance, a policy might specify that a critical application should always have a certain minimum amount of resources, or that non-essential tasks should be allocated less resources during peak usage times.
- Policy Enforcement: Once policies are set, z/OSMF can enforce them automatically. This involves monitoring the system's resource usage and adjusting resource allocation on-the-fly to adhere to the policies. For example, if a policy specifies a minimum resource allocation for a certain task, z/OSMF will ensure that this task always gets at least this amount of resources, reallocating resources from other tasks if necessary.
- Flexibility and Control: Policy-based management gives administrators a high degree of flexibility and control over resource allocation. They can set policies that align with their organization's specific needs, priorities, and goals. For instance, they might prioritize performance for certain critical tasks, while focusing on cost-efficiency for less important tasks. This allows the organization to get the most

value out of their system resources.

- Automatic Management: By enforcing policies automatically, z/OSMF can greatly simplify the resource management process. Administrators don't have to constantly monitor resource usage and manually adjust allocation; instead, the system does this for them, freeing up their time for other tasks.

Through policy-based management, z/OSMF's capacity provisioning feature can help ensure that resources are allocated in a way that aligns with the organization's needs and priorities, while also automating the resource management process to save time and effort.

5. Performance Monitoring and Adjustments:

PERFORMANCE MONITORING and adjustments form a critical aspect of z/OSMF's capacity provisioning features. By continuously evaluating and modifying system resource allocation based on real-time performance data, z/OSMF can ensure optimal system performance and efficiency. Let's discuss this in more detail:

- Performance Monitoring: z/OSMF is equipped with tools to continuously track the performance of various tasks and services within the system. It analyzes parameters such as CPU utilization, memory consumption, I/O operations, and more, and uses this data to understand the current system load and performance.
- Resource Adjustments: Based on the real-time performance data, z/OSMF can dynamically adjust the allocation of resources to different tasks or services. This ensures that resources are allocated in a manner that maximizes system performance and efficiency. For example, if a particular service is under heavy load and is identified as a performance bottleneck, z/OSMF can allocate more resources to it to enhance its performance. On the other hand, if a service is using more resources than necessary, z/OSMF can reduce its resource allocation and divert those resources to other tasks.
- Responsiveness: The performance monitoring and adjustments happen in real-time, making the system highly responsive to changes in load or usage patterns. This not only ensures optimal performance at any given time but also enables the system to effectively handle sudden spikes in demand.
- Virtual Resource Management: In addition to managing physical resources, z/OSMF can also adjust the parameters of

virtual resources based on performance data. For example, it can dynamically resize virtual machines or containers, adjust the allocation of virtual CPUs or memory, or change the priority level of virtual tasks.

Through continuous performance monitoring and dynamic resource adjustments, z/OSMF's capacity provisioning capabilities ensure that the system consistently operates at an optimal performance level, quickly responding to changes in load and efficiently utilizing resources.

6. Reporting and Analytics:

REPORTING AND ANALYTICS are essential for evaluating system performance, planning future capacity needs, identifying potential issues, and making informed decisions about resource allocation. Within z/OSMF's capacity provisioning feature, they serve several critical functions:

- Capacity Usage Reporting: These reports provide a detailed breakdown of how the system's capacity is being used. This includes information about which tasks or services are using the most resources, how resource usage varies over time, and how closely the actual usage aligns with the capacity that has been provisioned.
- Performance Metrics: z/OSMF tracks a variety of performance metrics that can provide insights into the efficiency of resource utilization and the overall performance of the system. This could include metrics such as CPU usage, memory utilization, I/O operations, response times, and more.
- Provisioning Activities: Reports on provisioning activities provide an overview of the changes made to the system's capacity. This includes details about when and how resources were allocated or de-allocated, which tasks or services were affected, and what triggered the change (such as a policy, a change in demand, a scheduled task, etc.).
- Analytics: Beyond simple reporting, z/OSMF also provides analytical tools that can help interpret the data and draw meaningful insights. For example, it can identify trends or patterns in the data, predict future capacity needs based on historical data, or use machine learning algorithms to identify anomalies that could indicate a problem.

- Usage in Capacity Planning and Performance Optimization: The reports and analytics provided by z/OSMF can play a crucial role in capacity planning and performance optimization. By understanding how resources are being used and how the system is performing, administrators can make more informed decisions about how to allocate resources, when to add more capacity, how to optimize system performance, and more.
- Troubleshooting: Lastly, the detailed reporting and analytics can also aid in troubleshooting. If there's a performance issue or an error, these reports can help identify the root cause and guide the troubleshooting process.

In summary, reporting and analytics in z/OSMF's capacity provisioning feature provide administrators with valuable insights into system performance and resource utilization, helping them to manage capacity more effectively and efficiently.

7.3 REST APIs in z/OSMF

THE REST APIS IN Z/OSMF allow other systems or applications to interact with z/OSMF programmatically. These APIs conform to the principles of Representational State Transfer (REST), a popular architectural style for web services. Let's dive deeper:

1. Interoperability: The REST APIs make z/OSMF interoperable with other systems and applications. This means that functions and tasks within z/OSMF can be performed not only through the web interface but also by sending HTTP requests from other systems or applications. This can enable automation and integration with other IT management systems.
2. Automation: By using the REST APIs, system administrators can automate various tasks and processes in z/OSMF. For example, they can script the creation of workflows, automatically adjust system parameters, or trigger incident reports.
3. Standardized Communication: The REST APIs use standard HTTP methods (like GET, POST, PUT, DELETE) and data formats (like JSON or XML), which are widely understood and used in the software industry. This can facilitate the integration with other systems and make it easier for developers to interact with z/OSMF.
4. Scalability: REST APIs are stateless, which means each request from a client to a server contains all the information needed to understand and process the request. This can help in scaling the system as it does not require the server to keep track of the state of its clients.
5. Security: The REST APIs in z/OSMF can also utilize security measures such as SSL/TLS encryption and HTTP

authentication methods to ensure that the data being transferred is secure and that only authorized systems or users can interact with z/OSMF.

6. API Endpoints: Each REST API endpoint corresponds to a specific function or resource in z/OSMF. For example, there might be endpoints for creating workflows, managing system configurations, or viewing incident logs.

In summary, the REST APIs in z/OSMF provide a way for other systems and applications to interact with z/OSMF programmatically, which can enable automation, integration, scalability, and security.

1. Interoperability:

THE REST APIS IN Z/OSMF play a critical role in system interoperability. In computing, interoperability refers to the ability of different systems, devices, applications, or products to work together and exchange information. This feature enables z/OSMF to integrate with a broad range of other software and hardware environments, promoting efficient data exchange and communication.

Let's delve deeper into the aspects of this interoperability:

- Integration with External Systems: One of the main benefits of the REST APIs is their ability to facilitate seamless integration with other systems or applications. For instance, you might have a third-party IT management system in your infrastructure. By using the z/OSMF REST APIs, this system can communicate with z/OSMF, send requests to it, and receive responses. This helps in creating a unified and well-coordinated IT environment.
- Automation: The REST APIs can be used to automate tasks in z/OSMF. For instance, instead of manually logging into the z/OSMF interface to perform a task, you can send an HTTP request to the corresponding REST API to perform the same task automatically. This can be particularly useful for repetitive tasks or tasks that need to be performed at regular intervals.
- Platform Independence: REST APIs are platform-independent, which means they can be accessed from any system or application that can send HTTP requests, regardless of the operating system or programming language used. This broadens the scope of integration and allows a diverse set of systems and applications to interact with z/OSMF.

- Streamlined Processes: By allowing external systems to interact with z/OSMF directly, the REST APIs can help streamline processes and workflows. Tasks that previously required switching between different systems or interfaces can now be done from a single point of control, improving efficiency and productivity.
- Standardized Communication: REST APIs use standard HTTP methods (like GET, POST, PUT, and DELETE) and status codes. This standardization makes it easier to build and maintain integrations with z/OSMF, as developers can leverage their existing knowledge of HTTP.

In essence, by enhancing interoperability, the REST APIs in z/OSMF can significantly improve the efficiency and versatility of your z/OS environment, enabling better integration, automation, and overall management.

2. Automation:

AUTOMATION, THE TECHNOLOGY by which a process or procedure is performed with minimal human assistance, is a key feature of the REST APIs in z/OSMF. It allows system administrators to automate various tasks and processes, leading to increased productivity, reduced human error, and a higher level of efficiency.

Below are more details on the ways automation is achieved through REST APIs:

- Scripting Workflows: Workflows are integral to system management, defining a series of tasks that lead to a final outcome. By using the REST APIs, administrators can automate the creation and management of these workflows. For example, a script can be written that sends HTTP requests to the z/OSMF REST APIs to create a workflow, add steps to the workflow, and execute it. This process can be triggered automatically at a specified time or based on specific system events.
- Automated System Adjustment: REST APIs can be used to automatically adjust system parameters. For example, a script could monitor the system load and, when it reaches a certain threshold, automatically send an HTTP request to the z/OSMF REST API to adjust system parameters and maintain optimal performance.
- Triggering Incident Reports: In the event of a system incident, REST APIs can be used to automate the process of logging and reporting the incident. For instance, when a system incident is detected, an HTTP request can be sent to the z/OSMF REST API to log the incident in the incident log, notify relevant administrators, and even initiate a workflow to address the incident.

- Integration with Other Automation Tools: The z/OSMF REST APIs can also be integrated with other automation tools or systems, extending their functionality. This could include anything from cloud management platforms to DevOps tools or scripting languages. By integrating with these tools, z/OSMF can become a part of larger, more complex automation processes.

Overall, the ability to automate tasks and processes through the z/OSMF REST APIs offers significant benefits, including saving time, reducing the possibility of human error, and enabling a more proactive and efficient approach to system management.

3. Standardized Communication:

REST, WHICH STANDS for Representational State Transfer, is an architectural style used for designing networked applications. A central feature of REST is its use of standard HTTP methods and data formats, which greatly facilitates communication and interoperability between different systems and applications. In the context of z/OSMF, this standardized communication offers several benefits.

- Ease of Integration: The use of standard HTTP methods and data formats means that z/OSMF's REST APIs can easily interact with other systems and applications, whether they're other IBM systems, third-party software, or custom-developed applications. This ease of integration makes it simpler to create a cohesive IT environment, where different systems can communicate and work together seamlessly.
- Familiarity for Developers: HTTP methods (like GET, POST, PUT, DELETE) and data formats (like JSON or XML) are widely used and understood in the software industry. This means that developers, regardless of their specific area of expertise, are likely already familiar with these standards and can therefore quickly learn how to use z/OSMF's REST APIs. This can reduce training requirements and make it easier to develop integrations or custom applications.
- Consistency: Using standardized communication methods also promotes consistency across different parts of the system or between different systems. This can make the system as a whole easier to manage and troubleshoot, as administrators and developers can apply the same knowledge and techniques across different areas.
- Interoperability: REST APIs are platform-independent,

which means they can be used with any programming language that supports HTTP, making them highly interoperable. This also ensures that z/OSMF can be accessed and manipulated from virtually any platform or device that can send HTTP requests, from servers and desktop computers to smartphones and IoT devices.

In sum, the use of standardized communication methods in z/OSMF's REST APIs greatly improves the system's flexibility, ease of use, and ability to integrate with other systems, thereby enhancing its value as a system management tool.

4. Scalability:

REST APIS ARE INHERENTLY stateless, which means that each request from a client to a server must contain all the information necessary to understand and process that request. This statelessness offers several benefits when it comes to scalability.

- Server Efficiency: As the server doesn't have to maintain any information about the client's state between requests, it can manage its resources more efficiently. This is because it doesn't need to dedicate memory or processing power to keep track of ongoing user sessions. As a result, the server can handle a larger number of requests simultaneously, improving the overall scalability of the system.
- Load Balancing: Since each request is independent and contains all the necessary information for processing, it can be handled by any available server. This allows for effective load balancing, as requests can be distributed evenly across multiple servers, further enhancing the system's ability to scale.
- Fault Tolerance: In a stateless architecture, if a server fails while processing a request, that request can be simply rerouted to another server without any loss of data or function. This enhances the system's resilience and availability, which are important aspects of scalability.
- Elasticity: In systems with REST APIs, capacity can be easily increased or decreased by adding or removing servers in response to demand. This elasticity makes it easier to scale the system up during periods of high demand and scale it down when demand is low, optimizing resource usage and cost.

In the context of z/OSMF, the statelessness of REST APIs means that the system can easily scale to manage larger z/OS environments or handle higher loads, making it a more flexible and cost-effective tool for system management.

5. Security:

THE REST APIS IN Z/OSMF can use several security measures to ensure secure data transfer and authorized access, which are crucial in any system management operation. Here's how these features enhance the security in REST APIs:

- SSL/TLS Encryption: SSL (Secure Sockets Layer) and TLS (Transport Layer Security) are cryptographic protocols designed to provide communications security over a computer network. They work by encrypting the data being transmitted, preventing unauthorized parties from intercepting or tampering with it. In the context of z/OSMF REST APIs, SSL/TLS encryption helps ensure that sensitive system management data is transmitted securely, even when it's sent over unsecured networks.
- HTTP Authentication: REST APIs in z/OSMF can use standard HTTP authentication mechanisms to verify the identity of the client making a request. This can involve techniques like basic authentication (where the client sends a username and password with each request), digest authentication (a more secure variant of basic authentication), or more complex methods like OAuth (which involves issuing tokens that grant specific permissions). This ensures that only authorized clients can interact with z/OSMF, helping to prevent unauthorized system management operations.
- API Key Management: Some implementations of REST APIs also use API keys, which are secret tokens that a client must provide when making a request. These keys are assigned to specific clients and can be used to track and control how the API is being used. This can provide an additional layer of

security by allowing administrators to limit what each client can do, revoke access if a key is compromised, or identify which client was responsible for a particular operation.

- Input Validation: REST APIs in z/OSMF should also validate all input received in requests. By checking that the input is in the expected format and contains valid values, the APIs can prevent injection attacks and other forms of malicious input.

By using these security measures, the REST APIs in z/OSMF can ensure that system management operations are secure, that sensitive data is protected, and that the risk of unauthorized or malicious actions is minimized.

6. API Endpoints:

IN THE CONTEXT OF A REST API, an "endpoint" is a specific URL where an API can be accessed by a client application. Every endpoint in an API corresponds to a particular function or resource that the API provides. For example, an API might have one endpoint for retrieving data, another for updating data, and so on.

In z/OSMF, each REST API endpoint corresponds to a specific function or resource. Here are some examples of what these might look like:

- Workflow Creation Endpoint: This endpoint could be designed to create workflows in z/OSMF. A client application could send a POST request to this endpoint with a body containing the necessary data for creating a new workflow. Upon receiving the request, z/OSMF would create the workflow and return a response indicating the outcome.
- System Configuration Management Endpoint: This endpoint might allow client applications to view or modify system configurations. For instance, a GET request could retrieve the current configuration data, while a PUT request could update the configuration with new values.
- Incident Log Viewing Endpoint: This endpoint would be used to access incident logs. A client application could send a GET request to this endpoint to retrieve a list of recent incidents. The API might also support filtering or searching incidents based on parameters included in the request.

The exact number and function of endpoints will depend on the specifics of the z/OSMF system and the tasks it's designed to perform. Importantly, each of these endpoints would use standard HTTP methods (GET, POST, PUT, DELETE, etc.), and would interact with data in standard formats like JSON or XML, allowing them to easily integrate with various other systems and tools.

Overall, the design of these API endpoints allows for a wide range of management tasks to be performed programmatically, enabling powerful automation and integration capabilities.

Chapter 8: Security and Compliance

Chapter 8, "Security and Compliance," delves into the fundamental security features and controls of z/OSMF. This chapter will guide you through critical security concepts, methodologies, and how to manage regulatory compliance within the framework. The two key areas covered include:

8.1 Role-Based Access Control This section discusses how z/OSMF implements role-based access control (RBAC), a method of regulating access to system resources based on the roles of individual users within the organization. In essence, RBAC assigns system access rights and permissions to users according to their roles, thus enhancing security, managingability, and efficiency.

8.2 Auditing and Compliance Management In this section, the emphasis is on how z/OSMF aids in achieving regulatory compliance and effective audit management. It includes details on auditing capabilities such as system logs, incident reports, and other resources to help monitor system activities. The section also covers how these tools can be utilized to demonstrate regulatory compliance, a critical concern for many organizations in fields like finance, healthcare, and other regulated industries.

8.1 Role-Based Access Control

ROLE-BASED ACCESS CONTROL (RBAC) in z/OSMF is a security model where access permissions are associated with roles, and users are assigned appropriate roles. Here's an outline of the main aspects:

1. Role Definition: In RBAC, a role represents a set of permissions that specify the operations that can be performed within the system. For example, a role might have permissions to create workflows, view system logs, or modify system configurations. The first step in implementing RBAC is to define these roles according to the needs and structure of the organization.

2. User Assignments: Once roles are defined, users are assigned to these roles. Each user can be assigned one or more roles, depending on their responsibilities. For example, a system administrator might be assigned a role that includes all permissions, while a regular user might be assigned a more limited role.

3. Role-Permission Relationship: The relationship between roles and permissions in RBAC is many-to-many. This means that a single role can have multiple permissions, and a single permission can be associated with multiple roles. This flexibility makes it easy to manage access controls in a way that suits the organization's needs.

4. Secure Operations: Once RBAC is set up, the system checks the user's roles and their associated permissions before allowing any operation. If the user's roles include the necessary permissions, the operation is allowed; otherwise, it is denied. This ensures that users can only perform actions that they're authorized to do.

5. Access Review and Update: Roles and user assignments should be reviewed periodically to ensure that they still fit the organization's needs and security requirements. Changes in job responsibilities, staff turnover, or changes in the system itself may require updates to the RBAC settings.

6. RBAC Benefits: RBAC can greatly enhance the security of a system like z/OSMF. It simplifies the management of permissions, making it easier to prevent unauthorized access to the system. It also provides more granularity in access control, making it possible to fine-tune access permissions according to the needs of the organization.

1. Role Definition:

IN THE CONTEXT OF ROLE-Based Access Control (RBAC), a role is a symbolic representation of a set of permissions that grants a user the ability to perform certain actions within a system. These permissions delineate the operations a user assigned to that role can perform. The capabilities can range from high-level administrative privileges to limited task-specific functions.

Defining roles is the first step in implementing an RBAC system. Roles should be constructed in alignment with the organizational structure and operational needs of the enterprise. Each role should encapsulate the privileges necessary to perform a specific job function. For instance, in a z/OSMF system:

- Administrator Role: This role might have wide-ranging permissions, including the ability to create workflows, manage system configurations, view and manage incident logs, install plug-ins, and more. The administrator role is usually reserved for high-level IT staff responsible for maintaining the z/OSMF environment.
- Operator Role: This role may possess more constrained permissions, allowing for tasks like executing workflows, monitoring system status, and addressing basic incident logs. This role might be suitable for IT personnel tasked with day-to-day management of the mainframe.
- Developer Role: This role could have permissions to create and test workflows, use the REST APIs, and access logs relevant to their tasks. It would be appropriate for software developers working in the z/OS environment.

Role definition should be approached with careful consideration. It is crucial to strike a balance between operational efficiency and security; roles should be designed to give users enough permissions to perform their duties effectively without granting unnecessary access. This principle is known as "least privilege" and is a fundamental concept in IT security. After the roles have been defined, they can be assigned to users, offering a structured, manageable approach to access control in the z/OSMF system.

2. User Assignments:

ONCE ROLES HAVE BEEN meticulously defined, the next step in implementing Role-Based Access Control (RBAC) is the assignment of users to these roles. Users are given one or more roles based on their job responsibilities and the level of system access they require to fulfill those duties. This allocation of roles serves as an effective way to control what actions each user can execute within the z/OSMF system.

For example:

- A System Administrator, typically responsible for overseeing the entire z/OSMF environment, might be assigned a role (or roles) with extensive permissions, allowing them to create workflows, modify system configurations, manage incident logs, and perform other necessary high-level tasks.
- A regular user, who might be an operator or a developer, would likely be given a role with fewer permissions, tailored to their specific duties. An operator, for instance, might have the role allowing them to execute and monitor workflows, while a developer may have access to create, test, and debug workflows and utilize REST APIs.

The process of user assignment must be done thoughtfully and securely. In practice, a user should only be given the roles and, by extension, the permissions needed to perform their job tasks effectively. This complies with the principle of least privilege, a key security guideline that dictates that users should have the minimum levels of access needed to accomplish their tasks.

This method of user assignment based on roles contributes to the security and compliance of the system. It simplifies the management of user permissions, provides a systematic approach to control access, and ensures that unauthorized or inadvertent access to critical system functions is minimized.

Furthermore, by associating permissions with roles rather than individual users, it becomes significantly easier to manage situations where job functions change, new functions are added, or when a user leaves the organization. In such cases, roles can be re-assigned or updated without the need to adjust permissions for each user individually.

3. Role-Permission Relationship:

IN THE ROLE-BASED ACCESS Control (RBAC) system, roles and permissions have a many-to-many relationship. This means that a single role can be associated with multiple permissions, allowing users assigned to that role to perform a variety of tasks. Conversely, a single permission can be tied to multiple roles, meaning that diverse roles could share a common permission.

For example, a role such as 'System Administrator' might have permissions to create workflows, modify system configurations, manage users, and perform other high-level tasks. At the same time, the permission to 'create workflows' might be associated with other roles too, like 'Workflow Developer' or 'Project Manager'. This structure allows the system to reflect the reality of complex business processes where different roles may share some responsibilities.

The many-to-many relationship between roles and permissions in RBAC provides great flexibility and granularity in managing access controls. It allows for a high degree of customization to tailor the access control system precisely to an organization's structure and needs. This also makes it easier to modify and update as organizational roles and permissions evolve over time.

Having such a system not only enhances operational efficiency but also contributes to maintaining the security of the system. When permissions are bound to specific roles rather than individual users, it becomes easier to audit access controls and ensure that users only have the permissions they need, reducing the risk of unauthorized or inappropriate access. This granularity also simplifies the task of updating permissions if a user's role within the organization changes.

4. Secure Operations:

IN AN RBAC MODEL, SECURE operations are maintained by system controls that regulate user activity based on their assigned roles and the permissions associated with those roles. Here's how this works:

- When a user attempts to perform an operation (like modifying a configuration, executing a workflow, etc.), the system first identifies the user and the roles they've been assigned.
- The system then checks the permissions associated with the user's assigned roles to determine if the attempted operation is within the user's granted access.
- If the user's roles do not have the necessary permissions for the operation, the system denies the operation. This prevents unauthorized or unintended actions from being carried out.
- If the user's roles do include the required permissions, the operation is allowed to proceed.

This form of access control provides a high degree of security and operational control, as it restricts operations to only those users who have been explicitly granted the appropriate permissions via their roles. It simplifies management of user privileges and ensures each user can only perform tasks pertinent to their role within the organization, thereby minimizing the potential for security breaches or misuse of the system.

Moreover, by employing this structure of permissions, an organization can more effectively comply with various regulatory requirements that demand strict control over who has access to certain types of data and operations. This could be particularly relevant for industries such as healthcare or finance where data privacy and security are paramount.

5. Access Review and Update:

REGULAR REVIEWS AND updates of roles and user assignments are crucial aspects of maintaining the security and efficiency of any system utilizing Role-Based Access Control (RBAC). The main objectives of these reviews can be categorized as follows:

- Ensuring Security: The primary aim of these reviews is to confirm that the current RBAC settings align with the organization's security policies. For instance, a user may change roles within the organization and no longer require access to certain sensitive information. In such cases, their previous permissions should be revoked to prevent unnecessary access. Regular reviews can identify such instances and prevent potential security vulnerabilities.
- Adapting to Organizational Changes: As organizations evolve, their structure and needs change. New roles may be introduced, certain roles may be altered or become redundant, and the responsibilities of existing roles may shift. Regular access reviews ensure that the RBAC setup mirrors the current organizational structure and requirements.
- Compliance with Regulations: Many industries are subject to regulations requiring them to periodically audit their access controls and make the results available for external review. Regular access reviews help meet these compliance requirements.
- Identifying and Correcting Mistakes: No system is immune to human error. Regular reviews provide an opportunity to identify and correct any mistakes in role definitions or user assignments, such as a user being assigned incorrect roles, or a role being given incorrect permissions.

The frequency and specifics of these reviews will depend on factors such as the size and nature of the organization, the sensitivity of the data being accessed, and the regulatory requirements that the organization is subject to. However, as a best practice, they should be carried out on a regular basis and whenever significant changes occur within the organization or its IT systems.

6. RBAC Benefits:

THE USE OF ROLE-BASED Access Control (RBAC) can greatly contribute to enhancing the security and overall management of a system such as z/OSMF. The benefits can be enumerated as follows:

- Simplified Permission Management: Instead of assigning permissions directly to each user, administrators can assign roles, which come with a predefined set of permissions. This not only simplifies the process of assigning and managing permissions but also ensures consistency in permissions for users with similar job functions. This approach also makes it easier to handle changes like new hires, terminations, or job role changes, as it's often a matter of simply updating the roles a user is assigned to.
- Enhanced Security: RBAC can reduce the risk of unauthorized access or actions within the system. By defining roles according to job function, users are only granted the permissions necessary to fulfill their responsibilities, minimizing the potential damage from user errors or malicious activities. This principle is often referred to as the principle of least privilege.
- Granular Access Control: RBAC provides more granularity in access control compared to traditional access control models. By allowing permissions to be grouped and assigned via roles, it becomes possible to fine-tune who has access to what and under which circumstances. This allows for a more flexible and precise implementation of the organization's security policies.
- Improved Auditability: By standardizing access across users with the same roles, RBAC simplifies auditing of user rights and helps identify anomalies or inappropriate permissions.

Moreover, RBAC can aid in regulatory compliance by providing clear documentation of who has access to sensitive data and why, which is often a requirement in various regulatory standards.

- Scalability: RBAC models scale well as an organization grows. As new roles are created or existing roles are expanded, permissions can be adjusted in a structured manner. This eliminates the need to manage access rights for each individual user, which can become unmanageable in large organizations.

Overall, implementing RBAC can lead to a more secure, scalable, and manageable system, with streamlined operations and improved compliance with internal policies and external regulations.

8.2 Auditing and Compliance Management

AUDITING AND COMPLIANCE management in z/OSMF is focused on ensuring that the system and its users adhere to certain rules and regulations, which could be internal policies, industry standards, or legal requirements. Here are the key aspects:

1. Activity Logging: In z/OSMF, all significant user activities and system events are logged. These logs can be reviewed to verify what actions were performed, by whom, and when. This information is crucial for both troubleshooting and auditing.

2. Audit Trails: Audit trails are records of chronological activities that provide documentary evidence of the sequence of activities that have affected a specific operation, procedure, or event. They provide a means to backtrack from an end event to the initiating event.

3. Compliance Reporting: Compliance reporting involves generating reports that demonstrate the system is in compliance with certain standards or regulations. For example, a report might show that all users have the necessary permissions and no more, demonstrating compliance with the principle of least privilege.

4. Intrusion Detection and Prevention: If the system detects an unusual or unauthorized activity, it can generate alerts. These alerts could lead to immediate action, such as blocking a user or initiating a security audit.

5. Regular Audits: Regular audits involve systematically inspecting the system and its operations to verify that they're in line with established policies and standards. This could involve checking user permissions, verifying the integrity of system data, or validating compliance with specific regulatory standards.

6. Remediation: If an audit reveals a problem, such as a user with excessive permissions or a discrepancy in system data, the issue can be remediated. Remediation might involve modifying user roles,

correcting data, updating system configurations, or potentially even disciplinary action against users if intentional misconduct is found.

In sum, auditing and compliance management in z/OSMF is about both verifying that the system is operating as it should and that it is following all the necessary rules and regulations.

1. Activity Logging:

ACTIVITY LOGGING IS a fundamental aspect of maintaining security and compliance within z/OSMF. The concept revolves around the recording of all significant user activities and system events. These can range from a simple login or logout of a user to more complex actions such as initiating workflows, changing system configurations, or managing incidents. Here are some more detailed points:

- Detailed Records: The logs contain detailed records of all actions that have taken place within the system. This includes who performed the action, what the action was, when it was performed, and often where it was performed from. The logs can also record any errors or issues that arose during the action.
- Error Diagnosis: The ability to review logs is particularly important when troubleshooting. If an issue arises within the system, the logs can provide valuable information about what led up to the problem. They can help identify what actions were taken just before the problem occurred and who performed those actions, offering significant clues that can aid in diagnosing and fixing the issue.
- Auditing and Compliance: From a compliance perspective, logs are essential for auditing. They provide an auditable trail of actions that can be used to prove compliance with various rules and regulations. For example, if you need to prove that certain checks or procedures were followed, the logs can provide that evidence.
- Incident Investigation: In case of a security incident, logs are crucial for investigations. They can help identify what actions were taken by an attacker, how they gained access, and what data or systems were affected.

- User Accountability: Finally, logs promote accountability. Knowing that all actions are being recorded can deter unauthorized or inappropriate actions.

Given the importance of logs, it's crucial to have a robust log management strategy in place, which includes secure log storage, efficient log retrieval, and regular log reviews.

2. Audit Trails:

AUDIT TRAILS IN Z/OSMF are essentially a more detailed and comprehensive form of activity logging. They provide a complete and chronological record of activities and events that have transpired within the system. Here are some key points to elaborate on this feature:

- Detailed Records: Much like activity logs, audit trails record detailed information about every activity. However, audit trails often include more context and metadata, allowing for a more comprehensive understanding of each event. This could include details like the initial conditions before an event, the inputs that led to it, any system responses, and the final outcomes.
- Traceability: The chronological nature of audit trails allows for excellent traceability. This means that you can follow the trail of activities from any point back to its origin. This is particularly useful for identifying the root cause of any problems or irregularities, as well as for understanding the series of events that led to a particular outcome.
- Compliance and Accountability: Audit trails are particularly important for compliance and accountability. They provide a record of who did what and when, which can be used to hold individuals accountable for their actions. In many industries, maintaining detailed audit trails is a regulatory requirement, as they can prove that the organization is complying with relevant laws and standards.
- Security Analysis: Audit trails are also a critical tool for security analysis. In the event of a security breach, they can help identify what actions the attacker took, how they were able to penetrate the system, and what data or resources they

accessed. This can be crucial for both remediation and future prevention efforts.

- Forensic Readiness: With cyber threats becoming more sophisticated, forensic readiness is a vital aspect of any organization's security strategy. Audit trails enable this by providing essential data for forensic investigations, ensuring that the organization can respond effectively to security incidents.

Overall, audit trails in z/OSMF provide a comprehensive and traceable record of all significant activities, enhancing security, accountability, and compliance.

3. Compliance Reporting:

COMPLIANCE REPORTING in z/OSMF refers to the process of creating and maintaining reports that validate the system's adherence to certain standards, regulations, or internal policies. This feature is essential for maintaining the transparency and integrity of the system. Here are some key points to elaborate on this feature:

- Demonstration of Compliance: Compliance reports demonstrate that the system and its administrators are following the required guidelines, laws, or industry standards. This could include regulations related to data security, user access controls, software and hardware management, or incident handling procedures. By generating these reports, z/OSMF can provide concrete evidence that it is being managed in a compliant manner.
- Validation of Controls: Compliance reporting is also useful for validating the effectiveness of the controls put in place within z/OSMF. For example, a report could show that role-based access controls are effectively limiting user access to data and functions based on their assigned roles. This helps validate the efficiency and security of the system.
- Regulatory Requirements: For many organizations, compliance reporting is not just a best practice—it's a regulatory requirement. Regulatory bodies often require organizations to submit compliance reports to demonstrate that they're maintaining the necessary security and management standards. With z/OSMF, creating these reports can be an automated and streamlined process.
- Insights for Improvement: Beyond simply proving compliance, these reports can also provide valuable insights that can be used to improve the system. By studying

compliance reports, administrators can identify areas where the system may be falling short of standards or expectations and take proactive steps to improve.

- Stakeholder Assurance: Finally, compliance reports can provide assurance to stakeholders, including customers, partners, and auditors, that the system is well-managed and compliant with all necessary regulations. This can enhance trust and confidence in the system and the organization as a whole.

In conclusion, the compliance reporting functionality in z/OSMF is a powerful tool for maintaining the system's integrity, improving its performance, and demonstrating adherence to necessary regulations and standards.

4. Intrusion Detection and Prevention:

INTRUSION DETECTION and prevention is a critical part of z/OSMF's security infrastructure. The system continuously monitors for suspicious activity that could indicate a potential security breach or malicious activity. Here's a deeper look at how this works:

- Detection Mechanisms: The z/OSMF system uses a combination of anomaly-based and signature-based detection mechanisms to identify potentially malicious behavior. Anomaly-based detection involves identifying behavior that deviates significantly from normal user activity, while signature-based detection involves identifying behavior that matches known patterns of malicious activity.
- Real-time Monitoring: z/OSMF continuously monitors all activities and events happening within the system in real-time. This includes user actions, system changes, data access, network traffic, and more. This real-time monitoring enables quick detection of potential intrusions or unauthorized activities.
- Alert Generation: When the system detects potential intrusion or malicious activity, it generates an alert. The alert provides details about the suspicious activity, including what occurred, when it happened, and who was involved. These alerts can be configured to be sent to administrators or a security team immediately, enabling them to take rapid action.
- Automatic Preventative Actions: In addition to alerting administrators, the z/OSMF system can also be configured to take automatic action in response to detected intrusions. This might include temporarily locking a user account, blocking an IP address, or disabling certain system functions. These

automatic actions can help to limit the potential damage caused by an intrusion.

- Regular System Auditing: Intrusion detection and prevention also involves regular auditing of the system to identify any potential weaknesses or vulnerabilities. This could involve checking for weak passwords, analyzing system logs for suspicious patterns, or scanning the system for known vulnerabilities.

In summary, intrusion detection and prevention in z/OSMF plays a vital role in protecting the system against unauthorized access and potential security breaches, ensuring the security and integrity of the system and its data.

5. Regular Audits:

REGULAR AUDITING IS a vital part of maintaining security and compliance in any system, including z/OSMF. Audits are a proactive measure that involve a thorough examination of various aspects of the system, its operations, and its security measures. Here's a closer look at what this involves:

- User Permissions: One crucial part of an audit involves examining user permissions. This means ensuring that each user has the appropriate permissions for their role and that unnecessary or excessive permissions aren't granted. The principle of least privilege, which states that users should only have the permissions they need to perform their tasks, is a key guide in this process.
- Data Integrity: Audits also involve checking the integrity of system data. This can involve verifying that data hasn't been modified unexpectedly, that backup procedures are working correctly, and that data is being managed in line with policies and regulations.
- Policy Compliance: Auditing involves checking that the system and its users are adhering to established policies. This could involve, for example, checking that password policies are being followed, or that data retention policies are being correctly applied.
- Regulatory Compliance: For systems that handle sensitive data or are used in regulated industries, audits will often involve checking for compliance with specific regulatory standards. This might include standards like GDPR for data protection, PCI-DSS for payment card data, or HIPAA for health information.
- Audit Records: An essential part of the auditing process

involves maintaining records of what was checked, what was found, and what actions were taken in response. These audit records can be important for demonstrating compliance, for future reference, and for identifying patterns or trends.

Regular audits are a best practice for system management and a critical tool for maintaining security, ensuring compliance, and promoting accountability. By identifying potential issues before they become problems, audits can greatly improve the overall security and efficiency of a system like z/OSMF.

6. Remediation:

REMEDIATION IS THE process of addressing and correcting issues discovered during audits or through other security measures. It's a crucial aspect of maintaining the overall security, integrity, and compliance of the z/OSMF system. Here are the details:

- User Roles Modification: If an audit reveals that a user has excessive permissions or has access to resources that are not necessary for their role, remediation might involve modifying the user's roles and permissions. This could mean removing a user from a particular role, adjusting the permissions associated with a role, or perhaps creating a new role that better suits the user's needs.
- Data Correction: If discrepancies or errors in system data are found during an audit, remediation will involve correcting this data. This could mean updating records, removing duplicates, or other forms of data cleaning. If the errors are the result of a systemic issue, such as a bug in the system or a misconfigured setting, further steps may be needed to address the underlying issue.
- System Configuration Updates: Remediation can also involve making changes to system configurations. If an audit finds that certain configurations are not in line with best practices, are causing performance issues, or are leading to security vulnerabilities, those configurations may need to be updated.
- Disciplinary Action: In cases where intentional misconduct is found, such as a user deliberately misusing their access privileges, remediation may need to include disciplinary action. This could mean revoking the user's access, initiating a formal disciplinary process, or even involving law enforcement in extreme cases.

- Prevention Measures: Beyond addressing the immediate issue, remediation also often involves implementing measures to prevent the issue from recurring. This could involve updating policies, improving training, adjusting audit procedures, or enhancing monitoring capabilities.

Remediation is all about not just responding to issues, but learning from them to improve the system's security and operations moving forward. It's about making the system more robust and resilient so that it's better equipped to handle the challenges and threats of the modern IT landscape.

Chapter 9: Troubleshooting and Maintenance

Chapter 9 of this guide focuses on the vital aspects of troubleshooting and maintenance in z/OSMF:

9.1 Common Problems and Solutions: This section is designed to help administrators deal with common problems that may arise while using z/OSMF. Each topic will introduce a typical issue, discuss its potential causes, and propose solutions or best practices to address it. Topics could range from connectivity issues and user access problems to difficulties in configuration and performance degradation.

9.2 Updating and Patching z/OSMF: Keeping z/OSMF up to date is crucial for the smooth functioning of the system, and for maintaining its security. This section will guide administrators on how to properly update z/OSMF and apply patches. Topics will include understanding release notes, the update process, potential pitfalls during an update, and verification of successful updates.

Overall, this chapter aims to provide administrators with a resource to refer to when they face difficulties with z/OSMF, and also guide them on the important task of keeping the system up-to-date and secure.

9.1 Common Problems and Solutions

THE "COMMON PROBLEMS and Solutions" section is intended to serve as a practical guide to help troubleshoot common issues that may arise when using z/OSMF. This section includes the following aspects:

1. System Startup Issues: Problems related to starting up the z/OSMF server, such as errors during startup or the server failing to start at all. Solutions might involve checking the system logs for errors, verifying the server configuration, or ensuring that all necessary resources are available.
2. Network Connectivity Issues: Issues related to network connectivity, such as being unable to access the z/OSMF web interface. Solutions could involve checking network settings, verifying that the network is operational, or diagnosing issues with firewalls or proxies.
3. Authentication Problems: Problems related to user authentication, such as users being unable to log in. Solutions might involve checking the configuration of the authentication system, verifying user account settings, or diagnosing issues with user credentials or access controls.
4. Performance Issues: Issues related to system performance, such as slow response times or high resource utilization. Solutions could involve checking system resource usage, optimizing configurations, or diagnosing issues with specific services or tasks.
5. Service Failures: Problems related to the operation of specific services or tasks, such as workflows failing to complete or incidents not being logged correctly. Solutions might involve checking the configurations of the affected services, diagnosing errors in workflows or tasks, or verifying the operation of dependent systems or services.

Each problem would typically be described in detail, including the symptoms, the potential causes, and step-by-step solutions to resolve the issue. This section serves as an essential resource for administrators to troubleshoot and resolve issues quickly and effectively.

1. System Startup Issues:

THESE ARE PROBLEMS that arise during the process of booting up or starting the z/OSMF server. Given the complexity of a z/OSMF system, there can be many reasons why a system might encounter startup issues. Below are detailed explanations of these issues and potential solutions:

- Startup Errors: During the startup process, the system might encounter errors that prevent it from starting successfully. These errors could be due to a variety of issues, such as incorrect system configuration, missing or damaged system files, or hardware issues. The exact nature of the error will typically be indicated in the system's error logs. By examining these logs, system administrators can identify the cause of the error and take appropriate corrective actions. This could involve modifying system configurations, replacing or repairing system files, or addressing hardware issues.
- Server Fails to Start: In some cases, the server might fail to start entirely. This could be due to serious system errors, hardware malfunctions, or other issues. In these cases, the first step is to check the system logs to identify any reported issues. If no issues are reported, or if the reported issues can't be resolved, it might be necessary to consult with IBM support or other experts for further assistance.
- Resource Availability: A z/OSMF server requires access to certain resources in order to start and function properly. This includes CPU time, memory, network access, and access to certain system files or databases. If any of these resources are unavailable, the server might fail to start. In these cases, the solution is to ensure that all necessary resources are available and accessible. This might involve freeing up memory or

CPU time, ensuring the network is functioning correctly, or checking the permissions and availability of necessary files and databases.

- Verification: Once the above issues are resolved, the server should be started again to verify that the problem has been corrected. If the server starts successfully, further testing should be conducted to ensure that all z/OSMF services are working correctly. If problems persist, the troubleshooting process will need to continue, possibly with the assistance of IBM support or other experts.

Ultimately, addressing system startup issues is a critical part of maintaining the availability and reliability of a z/OSMF system. While some issues can be resolved quickly, others might require in-depth troubleshooting or external assistance. However, with careful monitoring, regular system maintenance, and prompt troubleshooting, the impact of these issues can be minimized.

2. Network Connectivity Issues:

A KEY FEATURE OF Z/OSMF is its web-based interface, which requires network connectivity for access. Consequently, network issues can significantly impede the ability to manage and operate the system. Let's delve deeper into some common network-related problems and their potential solutions:

- Accessing the Web Interface: If users cannot access the z/OSMF web interface, this might be due to network issues. For instance, the server hosting z/OSMF may be down, or there may be issues with the network connection between the user's computer and the server. To troubleshoot this, administrators should first verify that the z/OSMF server is up and running. Next, they should test the network connection, which may involve pinging the server from the user's computer, or checking the network connection at different points between the user and the server.
- Network Configuration: Incorrect network settings can prevent z/OSMF from communicating with other systems or users. This includes incorrect IP addresses, subnet masks, or default gateway settings. Checking and correcting the network configuration can often resolve these issues.
- Operational Network: The network itself might be experiencing problems, such as a network outage or excessive network traffic that is slowing down the connection. Network diagnostic tools can be used to check the status of the network and identify any issues.
- Firewalls and Proxies: Firewalls and proxies can block network traffic between the user and the z/OSMF server. If a user can't access the z/OSMF web interface, administrators should check to see if a firewall or proxy is blocking the

connection. This might involve checking the firewall or proxy settings, or temporarily disabling the firewall or proxy to see if this resolves the issue.

- Secure Connection Issues: z/OSMF uses secure HTTP (HTTPS) for its web interface. If there are issues with the SSL/TLS configuration, such as an expired certificate or a mismatch between the server's certificate and its actual domain, users may be unable to access the interface. Administrators should check the server's SSL/TLS settings and its certificate to ensure that they are correct and up to date.

By taking a systematic approach to diagnosing and resolving network issues, administrators can ensure that users can access and use z/OSMF effectively.

3. Authentication Problems:

AUTHENTICATION IS A crucial aspect of security in any system, and z/OSMF is no exception. It ensures that only authorized users can access the system. Let's dive deeper into some common authentication-related problems and their potential solutions:

- Incorrect User Credentials: The most common reason for authentication failure is incorrect user credentials. If a user can't log in, the first thing to check is whether they're using the right username and password. They should be advised to check their input for typing errors, make sure their caps lock key is off (as passwords are usually case-sensitive), and try resetting their password if they think they might have forgotten it.
- Account Settings: If a user's credentials are correct but they still can't log in, there might be an issue with their account settings. For instance, their account may be locked due to too many failed login attempts, or it may have been disabled by an administrator. Checking the user's account status and adjusting the settings as needed can resolve these issues.
- Authentication System Configuration: z/OSMF supports several authentication methods, including RACF, LDAP, and others. If multiple users are having trouble logging in, there may be a problem with the configuration of the authentication system. In this case, administrators should verify the settings for the authentication method being used.
- Access Controls: Access control settings can also prevent users from logging in. For example, if a user has been removed from a role or their role no longer has the necessary permissions to access z/OSMF, they will be unable to log in. Administrators should review the user's role and permissions

to make sure they're correctly configured.

- System Clocks: Authentication might fail if the system clock of the z/OSMF server and the system clock of the user's machine are not synchronized, especially if Kerberos-based authentication is in use. Make sure both clocks are correctly set.
- Secure Connection Issues: If z/OSMF is configured to require secure connections (SSL/TLS), authentication could fail if there's an issue with the SSL/TLS configuration or certificate. Administrators should check the SSL/TLS settings and certificates to ensure they are correctly configured and up to date.

By correctly diagnosing and addressing these potential issues, administrators can ensure that users are able to authenticate successfully and gain access to z/OSMF.

4. Performance Issues:

SYSTEM PERFORMANCE is a crucial aspect of the user experience, and issues with performance can significantly impact the effectiveness of z/OSMF. Here are some common performance issues and potential solutions:

- High Resource Utilization: If the system is consistently using a high percentage of its CPU, memory, disk, or network resources, it can lead to performance issues like slow response times. Administrators should regularly monitor resource usage and identify any services or tasks that are using a disproportionate amount of resources. Once these have been identified, they can be optimized or, if necessary, allocated more resources.
- Misconfigured Settings: Sometimes, the system might be configured in a way that negatively impacts performance. For example, the system might be trying to perform too many tasks simultaneously, leading to resource contention. In this case, reviewing and optimizing the system configurations can help improve performance.
- Slow Network Connection: If the network connection between the user and the z/OSMF server is slow or unreliable, it can result in poor performance. Checking network performance and addressing any issues found can improve the user experience.
- Inefficient Code or Algorithms: Sometimes, a specific service or task within z/OSMF might be coded or structured in a way that's inefficient, leading to poor performance. If this is the case, optimizing the code or algorithm can make a big difference.
- Lack of System Maintenance: Regular system maintenance,

including updates and patches, is crucial for maintaining good performance. Outdated system components can lead to performance degradation over time.

- Hardware Limitations: In some cases, the system's hardware might simply be insufficient for the demands being placed on it. If the system consistently struggles to perform adequately even after other potential issues have been addressed, it might be necessary to upgrade the hardware.

By identifying and addressing these potential performance issues, administrators can ensure that z/OSMF runs smoothly and efficiently, providing a good user experience and effectively supporting the management of the z/OS environment.

5. Service Failures:

SERVICE FAILURES REFER to scenarios where specific functions or tasks within z/OSMF are not working as expected. This could include workflows not executing properly, incident logging not working, services becoming unresponsive, or even services crashing entirely. Addressing service failures often requires a thorough understanding of the service and its dependencies. Here are some common strategies for troubleshooting service failures:

- Reviewing Service Configurations: The first step when encountering a service failure is often to review the configuration of the affected service. Misconfigurations are a common cause of service failures. By verifying that the service is correctly configured, you can rule out this potential cause.
- Examining Log Files: Each service in z/OSMF typically maintains its own log file, which records details about the service's operation and any errors it encounters. Reviewing these log files can often provide crucial information about what went wrong and when.
- Testing Dependencies: Many services in z/OSMF depend on other services or resources to function properly. If a dependent service is unavailable or not functioning correctly, it can cause the service to fail. Testing these dependencies to ensure they're operating correctly can be an important part of diagnosing the problem.
- Reproducing the Failure: If possible, it can be helpful to reproduce the failure in a controlled environment. This can provide additional information about what triggers the failure, which can in turn provide clues about how to fix it.
- Updating or Patching the Service: Sometimes, a service failure can be caused by a bug in the service itself. If this is the

case, updating or patching the service to a newer version that fixes the bug might resolve the issue.

- Consulting Documentation or Support: If you're unable to diagnose or resolve the issue on your own, consulting the service's documentation or reaching out to IBM support can provide additional assistance.

By systematically working through these strategies, you can identify the cause of the service failure and implement a solution, ensuring that z/OSMF continues to operate effectively.

9.2 Updating and Patching z/OSMF

"UPDATING AND PATCHING z/OSMF" is a critical component of maintaining the functionality, security, and performance of your z/OS Management Facility. This section includes the following topics:

1. Checking for Updates and Patches: IBM periodically releases updates and patches for z/OSMF to fix bugs, add new features, and address security vulnerabilities. You should regularly check for these updates, either by monitoring official IBM communication channels or by using the built-in update checking functionality of z/OSMF.
2. Downloading Updates and Patches: Once an update or patch is available, you need to download it from the official source. This ensures that you're getting a legitimate update and not a potentially malicious file.
3. Applying Updates and Patches: After downloading an update or patch, the next step is to apply it to your z/OSMF installation. This typically involves stopping the z/OSMF server, applying the update or patch, and then restarting the server. You should always follow the provided instructions to ensure the update is applied correctly.
4. Verifying Updates and Patches: After applying an update or patch, you should verify that it has been applied correctly and that your system is working as expected. This could involve checking the version number of z/OSMF, performing basic functional tests, or monitoring the system for any issues.
5. Troubleshooting Update and Patch Issues: Sometimes, you might encounter issues when applying an update or patch, such as the update failing to apply or the system behaving unexpectedly after the update. In such cases, you should refer to the documentation for troubleshooting steps, or contact

IBM support for assistance.

Regularly updating and patching z/OSMF is critical to keeping your system secure, reliable, and up-to-date with the latest features and improvements. Always remember to follow best practices and guidelines to ensure the smooth operation of your system.

1. Checking for Updates and Patches:

THE PROCESS OF KEEPING z/OSMF up-to-date is an essential part of maintaining the system's security, performance, and functionality. IBM regularly provides updates and patches to z/OSMF that can address a variety of issues, including bug fixes, security patches, and enhancements or new features. To ensure z/OSMF remains optimal and secure, regular checking for these updates and patches is critical. Here's how to approach this:

- Monitoring IBM Communication Channels: IBM regularly communicates updates and patches through various channels like emails, newsletters, and their official website. By actively monitoring these channels, you can stay informed about the latest updates and patches available for z/OSMF.
- Using the z/OSMF Update Checking Functionality: The z/OSMF system itself often has a built-in feature that checks for updates and patches. This feature can be configured to periodically check for updates and notify you when they are available.
- Reviewing Release Notes: When updates or patches are released, IBM typically provides accompanying documentation, known as release notes, that detail the changes included in the update or patch. Reviewing these release notes can provide valuable insight into the problems that the update or patch addresses and any new features or functionality it adds.
- Establishing a Regular Update Schedule: Due to the critical nature of updates and patches, it's generally good practice to establish a regular update schedule. This schedule can ensure that you are consistently checking for and applying updates and patches, keeping your z/OSMF installation up-to-date

and secure.

While the specific process for applying updates and patches can vary depending on the nature of the update or patch and your specific z/OSMF installation, the general principle remains the same: regular checks and prompt application of updates and patches are key to maintaining the security, performance, and functionality of z/OSMF.

2. Downloading Updates and Patches:

THE PROCESS OF DOWNLOADING updates and patches for z/OSMF is a critical step in maintaining system security and performance. Ensuring that these updates are obtained from official, trusted sources helps protect your system from the risk of downloading and installing malicious files disguised as updates or patches. Here's a detailed explanation of this process:

- Official Sources: Always download updates and patches from official IBM sources. These could be the IBM Support website, official IBM download centers, or through direct links provided by IBM in their update announcements. This helps ensure that you're downloading legitimate files that haven't been tampered with.
- Verify File Integrity: IBM usually provides a way to verify the integrity of the downloaded files. This can be in the form of a checksum or a digital signature. By comparing the provided checksum or signature with the one you generate from your downloaded file, you can confirm that the file is genuine and hasn't been altered or corrupted during the download process.
- Secure Connections: Ensure you're downloading updates and patches over a secure connection. Look for the 'https' in your web browser's address bar, which indicates a secure, encrypted connection. This helps to protect the download from being intercepted or altered.
- Avoid Third-Party Sites: As a rule of thumb, avoid downloading updates or patches from third-party websites. These sites may not have the latest updates, and the files they provide can sometimes be bundled with unwanted software or, worse, malware.

- Record Keeping: It's good practice to keep a record of what updates and patches you've downloaded and installed, including when and from where. This can be helpful for troubleshooting purposes and for ensuring that you're keeping up with the latest updates.

The act of downloading updates and patches may seem simple, but it's important to take these steps to ensure the security and integrity of your z/OSMF system. Always ensure that your downloads are from trusted, official sources and that their integrity is verified.

3. Applying Updates and Patches:

ONCE YOU'VE DOWNLOADED the updates or patches from the official IBM sources and have verified their integrity, the next important step is applying these updates to your z/OSMF installation. Here's a more in-depth look at this process:

- Preparation: Before you start the update or patching process, make sure to read any provided documentation or release notes that come with the update. This will give you an understanding of what changes will be made and whether there are any known issues or prerequisites to consider.
- Backup: Before applying any updates or patches, it's crucial to create a backup of your existing z/OSMF installation and configurations. This is essential as it allows you to revert back to the previous state if something goes wrong during the update process.
- Stopping the Server: Usually, you will need to stop the z/OSMF server before applying an update or patch. This ensures that all system files are accessible and prevents any conflicts that might arise from changes being made while the system is running.
- Applying the Update: Follow the provided instructions to apply the update or patch. This process may vary depending on the update or patch, but it typically involves running specific commands or scripts provided with the update package.
- Verification: After applying the update, verify that the update was successful. This could involve running a verification tool, checking the version number of z/OSMF, or checking for new features or fixes.
- Restarting the Server: Once you have successfully applied the

update and verified it, restart the z/OSMF server. Monitor the system logs to ensure that the server starts up correctly without any errors.

- Post-Update Testing: Once the server is back online, perform some tests to ensure that everything is working correctly. This might involve checking that workflows still run correctly, that the interface is working as expected, and that other system functions are operational.

Each update or patch that you apply to z/OSMF is an important step in maintaining the security, stability, and functionality of your system. Always ensure to follow these steps carefully and diligently to ensure a successful update or patch application.

4. Verifying Updates and Patches:

AFTER AN UPDATE OR patch has been applied to your z/OSMF installation, the next crucial step is to verify that the changes have been successfully implemented and that the system is working as expected. This verification process includes several components:

- Checking the Version Number: The simplest way to verify that an update or patch has been applied is to check the version number of z/OSMF. The version number should reflect the latest update or patch that was installed. This can usually be found in the system's interface or through specific commands in the command line interface.
- Functional Testing: Functional tests involve running various tasks or functions of z/OSMF to ensure they are working correctly. This could include creating and running workflows, using the incident log management features, and more. These tests should be planned to cover all the main features of the system, especially those that were impacted by the update or patch.
- Performance Monitoring: After an update or patch, you should monitor the performance of the system to ensure that it's running as expected. This involves checking system resources, response times, and other performance indicators. Any noticeable decline in performance after an update may indicate an issue that needs to be addressed.
- Checking System Logs: System logs can provide valuable information about any potential issues with the update or patch. You should review these logs for any errors or warnings that occurred after the update was applied.
- Compliance Verification: If the update or patch was applied to meet certain compliance or security standards, you should

verify that the system now meets these requirements. This could involve running compliance checks or security scans.

Remember that the verification process is a vital part of maintaining the health and stability of your z/OSMF system. If any issues are discovered during this process, they should be addressed as quickly as possible to prevent further problems.

5. Troubleshooting Update and Patch Issues:

DESPITE ALL PRECAUTIONS, issues may arise when applying an update or patch to your z/OSMF system. These could range from the update failing to install properly, to the system exhibiting unexpected behavior following the update. In such scenarios, it's essential to troubleshoot these issues promptly to minimize disruption. Here are some key steps to follow:

- Reference the Documentation: Each update or patch released by IBM typically comes with associated documentation, which outlines known issues, troubleshooting steps, and fixes. This should be your first point of reference when encountering issues, as it likely contains information directly relevant to your situation.
- Review Error Messages: If the update or patch fails to apply, pay close attention to any error messages that are displayed or logged. These can provide valuable clues about what went wrong and how to address the problem. Common issues might involve file permissions, disk space, or compatibility issues with other software.
- Check System Logs: System logs can provide additional details about any issues that occur during or after the update process. You should review these logs for any entries related to the update or patch, as they can provide more context and help you understand what's going wrong.
- Test System Functionality: If the system is behaving unexpectedly after an update, perform functional tests to isolate the problematic behavior. This could involve testing different components or features of the system, or repeating specific actions to see if the issue occurs consistently.
- Contact IBM Support: If you're unable to resolve the issue on

your own, don't hesitate to reach out to IBM Support. Provide them with a detailed description of the problem, any error messages or log entries, and the steps you've taken to troubleshoot the issue. IBM's technical support team has in-depth knowledge of z/OSMF and can provide expert assistance.

Remember, updates and patches are crucial to maintaining the security, performance, and functionality of your z/OSMF system. It's important to address any issues that arise promptly to ensure your system remains in optimal condition.

Chapter 10: Future Directions for z/OSMF

10.1 Trends in Mainframe Management: This subsection would talk about the emerging trends and advancements in mainframe management and how they're expected to shape the future of z/OSMF. This could include trends such as increased automation, use of AI and machine learning, enhanced security measures, the integration of hybrid cloud environments, and more. Understanding these trends can provide insights into how z/OSMF needs to adapt to continue meeting the needs of its users.

10.2 What's Next for z/OSMF: This section would dive into planned or potential features and improvements for z/OSMF. This could be based on official roadmaps from IBM, insights from the user community, or speculation based on current trends. This could involve new features, improvements to existing features, changes in design or architecture, and more.

10.1 Trends in Mainframe Management

1. Automation: As with many areas of IT, automation is a key trend in mainframe management. This includes automating routine tasks, automating incident response, and using automation to improve efficiency and reduce errors. This trend is likely to continue and expand, with more and more tasks being automated.
2. AI and Machine Learning: The use of artificial intelligence (AI) and machine learning is increasingly being used in mainframe management. These technologies can help predict and prevent system issues, optimize system performance, and aid in decision-making processes.
3. Hybrid Cloud Environments: As organizations move towards hybrid cloud environments, mainframe systems need to be integrated and managed alongside cloud resources. This is a complex challenge that requires new approaches to mainframe management.
4. Security and Compliance: As cyber threats continue to evolve, so do the security measures to protect mainframe systems. Additionally, with new and changing regulations, compliance management is becoming more important.
5. Modern Interfaces and Accessibility: There's a trend towards providing more modern, web-based interfaces for mainframe management, like z/OSMF. This makes mainframes more accessible to administrators who may not have a traditional mainframe background.
6. Integration with DevOps: There's a growing trend to integrate mainframe operations with DevOps processes. This requires tools that can facilitate continuous integration/ continuous deployment (CI/CD) processes, automated

testing, and other DevOps practices on the mainframe.

These trends are reshaping the world of mainframe management, and it's expected that z/OSMF and similar tools will continue to evolve to support these new ways of working.

10.2 What's Next for z/OSMF

1. More Integration: Expect to see further integrations with other IBM systems and services. Integration with other mainframe tools and non-mainframe systems, especially those involved in hybrid cloud infrastructure, would make z/OSMF a more versatile and powerful tool for system management.
2. Expanded Automation: Given the trend in IT management toward automation, it's likely that future versions of z/OSMF will include expanded automation capabilities. This might mean more automated tasks, smarter automatic system adjustments, and better automated incident response.
3. Advanced AI Capabilities: With the rise of AI and machine learning, these technologies might be incorporated into z/OSMF for predictive analytics, anomaly detection, and system optimization.
4. Enhanced User Interface: As user experience is a critical factor in any software's success, future updates might include enhancements to the z/OSMF user interface, making it more intuitive, responsive, and easier to use.
5. Improved Security Features: With the ever-growing emphasis on cybersecurity, future developments will likely focus on strengthening z/OSMF's security features to ensure the system's integrity and the security of data.
6. Compliance Management: Given the increasing importance of regulatory compliance in many industries, we might see the introduction of new features aimed at facilitating compliance with various regulations.

REMEMBER, THESE ARE potential future directions based on trends and ongoing developments in mainframe management and IT in general. For the most accurate and current information on the future of z/OSMF, please refer to IBM's official communications and updates.

Appendix A: Glossary of Terms

1. z/OSMF: IBM z/OS Management Facility - A product for managing z/OS systems through a web browser interface.
2. Mainframe: A high-performance computer used for large-scale computing purposes where robustness, reliability, and scalability are of utmost importance.
3. z/OS: A 64-bit operating system developed by IBM for their z/Architecture mainframe computers.
4. Workflow: In the context of z/OSMF, a workflow is a defined series of steps to accomplish a specific task or set of tasks.
5. Plugin: A software component that adds a specific feature or service to an existing application.
6. API: Application Programming Interface - A set of rules and protocols for building and interacting with software applications.
7. REST API: Representational State Transfer API - A type of API that uses HTTP protocols to enable communication and data exchange between systems.
8. Capacity Provisioning: The process of allocating and managing resources in a mainframe environment to meet changing workload demands.
9. Role-Based Access Control (RBAC): A method of managing users' access to a system based on their role within the organization.
10. Incident Log Management: The process of recording,

tracking, and resolving incidents that occur in a system.

Appendix B: Useful Resources and Links

1. BM z/OS Management Facility (z/OSMF): The official page of IBM z/OSMF, where you can find product descriptions, features, and system requirements. You can access it here[1].
2. IBM Knowledge Center - z/OSMF: IBM's official documentation on z/OSMF. It provides comprehensive information on how to use z/OSMF, including task instructions, troubleshooting, and other topics. You can access it here[2].
3. IBM Redbooks - z/OSMF: IBM Redbooks provide in-depth technical content on IBM products and services. The z/OSMF Redbook can be a valuable resource for understanding and using z/OSMF. You can access it here[3].
4. IBM Developer - z/OS: A hub for developers working with IBM's z/OS, offering community, resources, and updates. You can access it here[4].
5. z/OSMF Forums: Online forums like IBM Developer Forums or Stack Overflow can be great places to connect with other z/OSMF users, ask questions, and share knowledge.

---

1. https://www.ibm.com/products/zos-management-facility
2. https://www.ibm.com/docs/en/zos/2.4.0?topic=services-zos-management-facility
3. https://www.redbooks.ibm.com/Redbooks.nsf/RedpieceAbstracts/sg248432.html?Open
4. https://developer.ibm.com/technologies/z-systems/

Epilogue

In this guide, we have walked through various aspects of IBM's z/OS Management Facility (z/OSMF), ranging from its basics to more advanced features. We've explored its installation process, interface navigation, system management capabilities, advanced features, security and compliance considerations, troubleshooting tips, and future trends.

IBM's z/OSMF represents a significant step in mainframe management, providing a web-based, integrated, and user-friendly interface that simplifies mainframe management tasks. Its rich features enable users to handle tasks such as incident log management, workflow management, system configuration, capacity provisioning, and more.

Through role-based access control, z/OSMF ensures the system's security and compliance while its capacity for extensions and plugins ensures it can be customized to cater to a wide range of needs. Troubleshooting is made easier through readily available resources and robust audit trails.

As mainframe systems continue to evolve and their management needs become more complex, tools like z/OSMF will continue to play a pivotal role in simplifying and streamlining these tasks. With its ongoing development and new features in the pipeline, z/OSMF is poised to remain an essential tool for mainframe management.

Whether you're new to z/OSMF or looking to deepen your understanding, we hope this guide provides a solid foundation and inspires you to explore further.

Don't miss out!

Visit the website below and you can sign up to receive emails whenever Isaac Nangan publishes a new book. There's no charge and no obligation.

https://books2read.com/r/B-A-SPRBB-IAQRC

Connecting independent readers to independent writers.

www.ingramcontent.com/pod-product-compliance
Lightning Source LLC
LaVergne TN
LVHW052302200926
848481LV00002B/443
* 9 7 9 8 2 2 3 0 2 0 5 8 5 *